Toyfolio

How to Invest in and Sell Toys Like Stocks

By
Greg Webb

DEDICATION

I want to dedicate this book to Kaylee, my wife,
who is always there for me.

Kaylee, I love doing life with you!

TABLE OF CONTENTS

ACKNOWLEDGMENTS

Thanks to my friend Trent who told me about Amazon and who continues to be a resource and mentor to whom I can always go.

Thanks to Barrington McIntosh, Lance Wolf, and Robert Travino for pushing me to write this book and for keeping me accountable. Thank you for the opportunity and platform to teach and serve others.

Toyfolio by Greg Webb

DISCLAIMER

This book offers broad advice on how to invest in and resell toys. Your results completely depend on your own decisions and practices.

INTRODUCTION

Have you ever been so nervous your stomach hurt? That was me in the fall of 2014. I was engaged to my now wife, who at that time was still an undergraduate. She was on track to graduate in May of 2015 and our wedding would follow in June. She was actively applying for graduate school at the time and hoped to start her graduate work in the fall. I realized that I was getting married in a matter of months, and I was only bringing home $35,000 a year. The thought of being the sole income and putting her through graduate school at the same time made my stomach churn with anxiety.

During this time, I started looking for ways to make additional income on the side. I had previously experienced some success selling old unwanted items from around the house, from my childhood, on Craigslist and eBay. I started to focus on how I could possibly scale that into something that was putting at least a couple extra hundred dollars a month in my pocket. At that time, that would be life-changing money.

The wildly popular movie *Frozen* had been released in November 2013, but no one in the toy industry realized just how popular it would be. With the late November released date in 2013, toys were scarce that year. By fall of 2014 the stores were well stocked, or so they thought.

All every little girl in America wanted in 2014 for Christmas was something *Frozen*. I started to notice all *Frozen* toys on eBay were selling like crazy, and so I decided to spend some of what I had in my savings account on anything and everything *Frozen*.

I wish I had a picture, because I had one particular Elsa doll, *THE* "Snow Glow Elsa", stacked to the ceiling. The popcorn ceiling in my house scratched one of the boxes! Elsa dolls to the ceiling. Maybe there is a rap song in there somewhere? Anyway, by Halloween, I was well stocked and that's when I would have a life changing conversation. It was just one of those moments in time that sticks with you forever and you remember every detail.

It was Halloween night and I was standing around talking with a couple friends when the topic of online businesses came up. I confessed that my spare bedroom looked like a winter wonderland with *Frozen* baby dolls, when my friend told me that he too was buying as many of the same items as I was as he could find. The only difference was that I was trying to sell them on eBay, and he was selling them on Amazon. I had never heard of people selling on Amazon. Is that really a thing? How does that work?

He told me that it was super fun, as well as easier and less work to sell on Amazon over eBay. On eBay, I had to create my own listings for every item that I wanted to sell. This included thinking of a creative title and captivating description, as well as taking eye-catching and quality pictures. Multiply this process by a large quantity of different SKUS and you had yourself a full-time job. On the other hand, my friend was scanning the UPC code on the product with his phone, hitting a few buttons, and boom; his product was listed on Amazon. No titles, no descriptions, no photos. The product page of the item already existed, so all he was doing was letting Amazon know he had some available. Better yet, instead of running to the Post Office every single day to ship items, he was sending them into Amazon FBA (Fulfillment by Amazon. More on this in Chapter 2), and never touching the product again. Too. Good. To. Be. True.

That conversation bothered me. Not that I was upset, but the kind of bothering that just sat on my mind and wouldn't go away. I knew I had to do something with that information. In the meantime, I temporarily suppressed that bothering feeling because I had work to do. I had *Frozen* merchandise to ship. I'll never forget having packages everywhere and staying up all hours of the night to tape up boxes and print out shipping labels every day through the middle of December. Christmas came and I was tired, but after all the fees and everything had cleared, I had put

That's when the conversation I had just two months prior came a couple thousand dollars extra in my pocket. It felt great. back to the front of my mind. A lot had happened in that two months and quite honestly, eBay had burned me out. The energy it took to constantly ship out orders was exhausting and the thought of continuing that day after day to make a side income didn't excite me. I went back to my friend and asked him to tell me more about Amazon. He told me no. What? No? He said he wouldn't talk to me anymore about it until I read a book called *Arbitrage* by Chris Green. So, I ordered the book and read it in two days. I don't use these words lightly, but it changed my life. I immediately picked up the phone again and called my friend. This time we met and went shopping for products. We walked around several stores that afternoon and he answered many of my initial questions.

By mid-January of 2015, I had my Amazon account all set up and I sent my first shipment into Amazon FBA just to test it out. To my surprise, within a week I had my first sale! I sold a Red Velvet pancake mix. No kidding. I bought it for $3 at Wal-Mart and sold it for $12. At that point, I was hooked, and I felt like I could conquer the world. Soon after my first sale, I found several clearance Batman belts for $9 at Wal-Mart. My Amazon app told me it was selling for $60 and I couldn't believe it. No way would someone in their right mind pay $60 for a plastic Batman belt with a couple plastic accessories. The 6 that I bought sold out in about two months, four for $60 and the other two for $90!

Since those days in 2015, I haven't sold many red velvet pancake mixes. Rather, I have exclusively focused on toys and video games. I wouldn't say that I am an expert on toys, but I do have a keen eye for them. I can walk into just about any retail store and tell you how long a particular toy has been on the shelf and what the price is on Amazon. If I don't, I can find out with the help of an app in about ten seconds. To me, toys are a currency of their own. Did you know that many toys increase in value over time? It's true. My mind is constantly blown at the astronomical prices that toys reach every year. Since discovering this truth, I have developed my own method of capitalizing on the toy market every year. In our community of sellers, we call it Buy and Hold 'em. It's like buying up stocks on a low and selling on a high, except with Legos and Barbies. You can invest in and sell toys just like stocks every year and this book will teach you how.

Now, I'm still a small fish when it comes to Amazon sellers. I don't sell millions of dollars' worth of items every year like many other sellers I know. I will get there one day because I still have so much to learn about the platform. But for now, I am content with slow and steady growth. For now, I still work full-time outside of my Amazon business. I enjoy doing both jobs, however, the Buy and Hold 'em strategy I will lay out in this book has allowed me to make more money selling part-time on Amazon, than I make full-time in my other occupation. While this book will mostly talk about selling toys on Amazon, you don't have to sell on that platform. The methods laid out here can apply to any platform you wish, including, but not limited to, eBay, Facebook Marketplace, Shopify, and more. It's just that at the time of this edition, Amazon has a distinct advantage that I will explain later.

The methods I lay out in this book are allowing me to achieve the ultimate goal I had in mind when I was a soon to be newlywed scared to death back in 2014: financial independence. I hope that is your goal as well. That's something that everyone can agree on and anyone can do. You just must take action. Thus, if you are an investor looking to diversify, a parent or grandparent looking to earn a side income online, a seasoned seller looking to implement a new strategy, or a newlywed scared to death and trying to make extra money, I challenge you to implement the strategies laid out in this book and let your portfolio look more like a ToyFolio.

Toyfolio by Greg Webb

1
WHAT IS A TOYFOLIO?

Caught ya. This book isn't one where you can skip the introduction. I know you used to do that back in literature class in high school and it became a bad habit, but I'll give you a few minutes to go back and get caught up because without it, you miss out on a lot of the context of the book going forward. No hard feelings, I'll wait.

...

There. Now we are caught up. No one on the planet was as excited about red velvet pancake mix as I was back then. Believe it or not, I saved a bag and it sits in my office as a humble reminder of where I started. It wasn't a huge profit, but it will always be my first Amazon FBA sale. If we want to talk profits, how about buying $9 Batman belts and selling them for $60-90!? While it was nice, I'll be the first to level with you that buying something and selling it for 10 times what you paid for it doesn't happen every day. But you can make some handsome margins with toys, year after year, that beat just about any investment out there.

Before I rattle anyone, I'm not here to attack the stock market. I have money in the stock market, and I think that everyone should have a diverse investment portfolio that spreads around the risk of investing. I have retirement accounts that I contribute to monthly just like many people around the world. Making profits with your Toyfolio is a perfect way to beef up your other forms of investing. To diversify your investments, I suggest building a Toyfolio in addition to a traditional portfolio of assets.

However, just like any other investment, don't put money at risk that you cannot afford to lose. You should not be spending your utilities money, retirement savings, or child's college fund on toys. Rather, set aside an amount you can afford to lose, stick with that amount, then continue to reinvest it as you make profits. Someone can implement the strategies in this book with as little as $500 to $1,000. I'll go over more specifics as to what it really takes to get started in Chapter 6.

Now, without getting into specifics and spending hours giving a dissertation of investment options and rates of return, when most people think of the "market" in the US, we are referring to the S&P 500 or the Dow Jones Industrial Average. These indexes are a collection of the largest publicly traded companies in America. For arguments sake, the market has averaged an 8-12% return since its inception. Some years it's much more, the most recent being in 2017 with a return of nearly 20%! In stark contrast, some years are much lower, such as in 2015 where the return was slightly in the negative. Overall, on average, you land in this 8 to 12% range for return on investment (ROI) including all the ups and downs. 8 to 12% ROI is nothing to sneeze at and is considered very healthy grow. Better yet, this money and interest compounds from year to year.

However, if you buy the right toys at the right price, like I will teach you in this book, it's not uncommon to make a 100% ROI every single time. Great days bring 200 to 300% ROI and on a bad day, 25% ROI is acceptable. In a worst-case scenario, you break even or lose a little. If I am totally honest, I have lost money on several toys over the past 5 years. 99% of the time it was due to either making the wrong buying decision or being impatient. Other times, I was taking a chance on an item and going in, I knew that losing money was a strong possibility. However, losing money on items has happened less often as I have perfected the strategy laid out in this book.

Now, just like in any business, the numbers do not always come out to a clean 100% ROI. Building a Toyfolio means operating a real online business that costs money. Buying boxes, insurance, subscription services, and other necessities will eat away at your profit margins. In Chapter 6, I will cover all the necessary expenses to which you'll need to pay attention, but for now the point I want to make is that if I have $10,000, I can get a better return selling toys than I can putting the same money into the traditional market.

Thus, a Toyfolio is the portfolio of toys you will buy and sell year after year for big profits. Like stocks, if you reinvest your profits, this method of investing can too compound from year to year. However, unlike investing in stocks, index funds, or mutual funds that passively make money, a Toyfolio is not passive. You can build a system where you are pretty much hands off, but it will require your energy, especially getting started. Having a Toyfolio is a hands-on investment. While you'll manage your assets online like you would traditional investment accounts, you will actually be handling physical toys.

You will be acquiring inventory by doing what Amazon sellers call Retail Arbitrage (RA) and Online Arbitrage (OA). RA is the process of going into brick and mortar stores and buying inventory that sells on Amazon or other platforms for more than your buy cost. OA is the process of finding items on other websites that you then can sell for a profit on other platforms. Later on, I'll get into more specifics as to how and why these methods work.

Now, when I mention selling physical products, some people immediately get turned off because they think they will have to start pitching random toys to their next-door neighbor or family members in hopes to make a sale. This is not how a Toyfolio works. A Toyfolio is not a multilevel marketing scheme where you have people above you or below you dependent on your sales. A Toyfolio is independently owning and operating a legitimate online business that consists of selling physical toys to real customers around the globe.

2
WHAT IS BUY AND HOLD 'EM?

When I first started my Amazon business in January of 2015, I joined a couple Facebook groups for Amazon and other e-commerce sellers. Everyone was still talking about Q4. What is Q4 you ask? Q4 stands for the fourth quarter of the year, better known as October through December. This quarter is considered the hottest sales time of the year. Those in the Facebook groups talked about it as if it was some long-lost nirvana. Everything about it seemed mystical and exciting. The Q4 of 2014 was gone though, and I had to look to the future. Thus, I was solely focused on finding more profitable items. Toys seemed like the easiest niche to really get started in. Grocery, Clothing, and Health and Beauty products were honestly more work. You cannot just throw a bottle of shampoo into a box with a bunch of other items. Grocery, Clothing, and Health and Beauty items always must be prepped in a special way, which primarily includes poly-bagging an item. Poly-bagging slowed my process down, which was a big deal because I was working this business around a full-time job. My only time to work on it was either very early in the morning or two to three evenings a week. Toys were much easier; just let Amazon know how many you had and then send them on their way.

I sold several toys throughout 2015, but then came Q4. In

December of 2015 my sales increased four times what they normally were. I sold $20,000 worth of products in December alone, with toys being the large majority of those sales. However, I sold out of many of the toys I had in stock in a matter of hours, not days. If you've never sold popular toys on Amazon during the middle of December, then there is no way to verbalize the velocity of the sales. I was *utterly* unprepared. On one hand, I was ecstatic. I had sold out of mostly everything! On the other hand, I was bummed. Many of the toys that I had in stock went on to reach prices that were double and triple the price at which I sold mine. I was flabbergasted. I would spend hours looking up random toys and giving my jaw a workout as it dropped over and over at the prices of what toys were selling for during the peak Christmas buying season.

I decided right then and there that I would be better prepared for Q4 of 2016. I was planning to have as much stock as I could possibly afford. This required an overhaul of my strategy that would become today's Buy and Hold 'em strategy.

The Common Way to Sell on Amazon.

As an Amazon rookie, I would go sourcing for products, bring those products home, prep them as fast as I could, then send them into Amazon FBA as quickly as possible. As was the problem then and now, most of the items I was sourcing were on clearance at major big box stores such as Wal-Mart and Target. This means that everyone selling on Amazon in the US was doing the *exact. same. thing.* The result? You have a huge surplus of sellers selling the same products all on the same listing. Basic economics teaches us that this is bad. Anytime you have a surplus of *supply*, especially from a variety of suppliers, price goes *down* because there is an excess of competition. This is especially true if the item wasn't necessarily an item in much *demand*. If the item wasn't wildly in demand, the result is that an item will plateau at a price point at which third-party FBA sellers are making pennies in an attempt to make a sale. Without a huge influx in demand, the price can stagnate for months, because the market is saturated with unwanted goods. Typically, this "rush to the bottom," as Amazon sellers like to call it, obviously results in Amazon customers getting a great deal on these items for a short window in time. Typically, after enough time, the price will stabilize and correct itself to where it was previously before the influx of sellers.

This is where it is important to understand Amazon's Best Seller Rank or *BSR*. In brief, Amazon assigns a rank to every item in its catalog for every category. There is a number one item in Toys, a number one item in Grocery, a number one item in Electronics, and so on. The best item obviously gets ranked number one, while the item that has either never sold or has sold the least gets assigned the last number in the category. Since the Toy category is smaller than the Book category, for arguments sake, the worst selling toy may be ranked 6,000,000, while the worst selling book may be ranked 62,000,000.

This rank is constantly moving and being updated. It's literally changing every minute of every day. Every time an item sells it moves down (closer to #1) in rank, while the more time that lapses without a sale, it moves up (away from #1) in rank. Thus, based on BSR, Amazon is telling us what is in *demand*. This is powerful information. In demand products were the products that I was watching in December hit astronomical prices. Surprisingly, many sellers do not understand the Amazon sales rank and how it directly relates to consumer demand, but I've built an entire strategy around it.

It got old fast to send in products as soon as I bought them and watch the price tank as sellers brutally undercut one another to get another sale. Plus, I didn't have time for that. I had limited time to shop for products around my full-time job and watching the prices on all my inventory drop to a price point where I wasn't making any money was extremely frustrating and made me feel as if my time was worthless. That's when I had to decide. Give up? After all, there wasn't much money to be made if every time I sent a product in the price would plummet. Or adjust? I chose the latter.

Buy and Hold 'em

While I sat in frustration, it dawned on me, all kinds of retail stores have *limited* shelf space. They are all governed by various rules and guidelines from manufactures and store policies to constantly be adding new products. This is especially true for toys. You do not see this as much in other departments. Wal-Mart is always going to have a white bath towel in the spot where white bath towels go. Target will always have a mixing bowl in the kitchen appliance section. While there are some generic toys (e,g., playing cards, building blocks, etc.) that are toy section staples, toys have huge turnovers every year because manufacturers are always trying to come up with something new and exciting that is going to stick and be *the* toy come Christmas time. Add in shelf space rotating multiple times a year, in conjunction with new movie releases or TV series, and you have a system where wildly in demand toys (based on their historical Amazon best-sellers rank) are on shelves for a very limited time, then once they are put on clearance, they are typically gone from store shelves…(in my *Sandlot* voice)…*For-ev-er.*

Let me say that again in case I wasn't clear. Wildly *in demand* toys are *deeply discounted* to make room for new inventory and clear shelf space. Once they are gone from store shelves, in many cases they will *never* see a store shelf again. The only place you will be able to find these toys is online, being offered by third party sellers on Amazon, eBay, Facebook Marketplace, or any other online selling platform. Talk about very limited supply! Thus, the limited supply factor coupled with Amazon's Best Seller Rank and customer demand, and you have a formula for BIG profits. You just have to buy the right products and exercise patience and discipline.

Therefore, when I see toys that are ranked really well on Amazon, selling for 75% off at Wal-Mart, my first thought *isn't* to see how quickly I can flip them. Even though in the moment it appears that I can make a decent profit, my experience tells me that by the time I can get them home, prepped, and sent into Amazon FBA, and by the time they are available for sale on Amazon, the price will have already dropped significantly due to other sellers trying to capture a sale. Thus, I assume the market will repeat this very cycle every time I buy an item, so I am patient. I *buy* as many as I can possibly find, even after prices on Amazon are not profitable, and I *hold* them until the market reaches wildly profitable prices. I know that if I hold toys long enough by exercising patience and delaying gratification, that it's only a matter of time before most of the other sellers are sold out. When this happens, I am holding a limited supply toy that still has a huge demand on Amazon because it's one of the very few places that you can still find the toy.

Using this information, I have built a system where I am constantly sending in products that I have been sitting on for three months, six months, a year, or sometimes over a year. Once you get the Toyfolio Buy and Hold process in place, you can sell items year-round that have far less competition at higher price points because in many cases, you control the market for the item.

The PRIME X Factor

It's nothing but remarkable the system that Amazon has built to deliver items around the world in as little time as they do. Americans are spoiled by it. Amazon has programs in major cities in America that allow us to order and receive items *within hours*. That is insanely powerful.

Amazon loves to sell us physical products, but their real business is customer service. They want to serve you so well and so quickly that you will only think about shopping online with them. For the most part, that is exactly what they have done. Only 10% of all retail shopping in America is done online and Amazon accounts for half of that online market! I'd say they are doing very well at gaining and keeping customers. They do this by building trust and serving you well. They get your product to you in a timely manner and if for some reason they make a mistake, they always go above and beyond to make it right.

Through their Prime membership program, they have trained Americans that they can get almost anything delivered to their doorstep in a matter of two days! At the time of this writing, they just announced that they are upping their game and making the delivery window for prime purchases one day. Again, just unbelievable.

Americans are conditioned to only use Amazon for online shopping because they know they will get the item they want within a reasonable amount of time. Even if the same item is cheaper at another online retailer, people still pay more on Amazon because they don't have to go through the hassle of creating another store account, they don't have to get endless emails from the other store, and they again get the item they want with no agitation in a timely manner. This has *huge* implications when it comes to the toy market.

Somehow, every year, we forget that Christmas comes on December 25th. It doesn't even change dates like Thanksgiving and Easter, yet every year people are dying to get last minute gifts for loved ones on Christmas Eve. You'd think that with the amount of technology and life enhancing services that we have available to us today, that we would be able to slow down and enjoy the holiday season with those we love. However, you know that many times the opposite is true. We run around from place to place and before we can blink, Christmas has come and gone.

Again, Amazon is in the customer service business. Americans rely on Amazon to serve them anything from toothpicks to prefab houses. Thus, when it comes to a 10-day window before Christmas, millions of people *only* shop on Amazon because they *trust* them to get their package to them in time. Amazon earns the right to be the only place people shop for Christmas in that 10-day window by "mundanely," delivering everyday purchases the other 355 days of the year.

We as third-party sellers get to leverage that trust through

Amazon's Fulfillment by Amazon (FBA) program. FBA means that third party inventory is sitting at Amazon fulfillment centers and Amazon handles all of the shipping and customer service responsibilities. Fulfilled by Merchant (FBM) means that the third-party seller plans to ship the item directly to their customer. On average, customers on Amazon will purchase an item from an FBA seller before an FBM seller, even if the price is higher. This is intensified during December because customers want assurance that they will receive their item on time.

During this critical time in December, it is inevitable that millions flock to Amazon to find those really popular toys that in many cases no longer exist on store shelves. This results in a perfect formula for you and me, especially if we have good FBA inventory ready. A huge customer demand, plus a limited supply item, plus complete trust that the customer will get the item they want in a timely manner, results in significant profits.

For most of your Buy and Hold items that you will purchase, this is your exit window. It's not uncommon to see items spike to three or four times their MSRP or historical selling price during December when customer demand is at its height. It's very easy to capitalize during this window of time and then have capital and profits to reinvest for the next year. In Chapter 4, I will show you how to know when to sell your items, but for now you need inventory to sell.

Toyfolio by Greg Webb

3
WHERE AND HOW DO I
FIND TOYS TO SELL?

The short answer is: everywhere. As you know, toys have entire departments in big box stores such as Wal-Mart and Target. Those two are the most popular stores that many e-commerce sellers source from simply because they are more widely available. The trick to sourcing toys well is understanding store mark down schedules. Certain times of the year can be exceptionally more profitable than others. Let's take a more detailed look at those two stores.

Target

Based upon my observations, Target does a mass clearance of toys twice year. The first typically occurs in January, which is when they clear out the huge surplus of toys left over after Christmas. Sometimes, they even start marking down toys the day after Christmas. The second major mark down almost always occurs in July. This occurs to make room for all the new toys they want to carry in their store for Christmas. Target also has their act together; in case you didn't know. They are strategic in everything they do. Just about every item that they put on clearance is a *nationwide* clearance. Meaning, everyone across the country is likely finding the same deals you are. Remember what

I said happens when everyone finds the same deals at the same time? Yep, prices on Amazon drop like a sack of rocks. Resist the urge to send in inventory immediately. Buy and Hold!

Target also follows a strategic mark down schedule. Items in each department of the store are typically marked down on a specific day of the week. At the time of this publishing, Thursday is toy day. Target also follows a 3-step mark down in most cases. The first mark down is typically 30% off. After a week or two, the second markdown is to 50% off. Lastly, three to four weeks from the initial markdown, the price will go to 70% off. Target has only recently started deviating from this schedule on big-ticket items, such as Legos and higher priced electronic toys. In those cases, they throw in a few more markdowns in between, which makes the markdowns a less dramatic decrease. These items start at 15% off then go to 30%, then to 40%, 50%, 60%, and lastly 70%. During the next example, we will stick to the more widely used schedule of 30% to 50% to 70%.

I want you to think of this markdown schedule as a stoplight. When the price is 30% off, the light is *red*. Do *not* buy. I know what you are thinking. "But I just scanned this 30% off item and it shows that I can make a great profit!" Look, I know it says that now, but tell me what the profit is after 3 days. I don't say that out of arrogance, I say that from experience. I am trying to *protect* you from making a bad purchase. The main reason why it is a poor choice to buy at 30% off is because there are hundreds of other sellers that will find the same item for 50%-70% off and undercut you in a heartbeat, leaving you left high and dry with zero profit margin for the foreseeable future. The *only* items that can be justified buying at 30% off are Legos and limited store exclusive items. I personally don't buy anything at 30% off, not even the limited supply stuff. There is just *so* much inventory that I could spend money on, so I am willing to wait for a better deal. I have a couple friends that buy Legos at 30% off, but they are also holding them long term. They even have a climate-controlled basement with dehumidifiers to store Legos in for 2-3 years. Talk about goals! When the price is 30% off, I want you to think of it as a time to scout. Go in, walk the toy section, scan items, but do not buy. Find the really good stuff and make a list of items that you want to buy when they get marked down again, so that you have a plan of attack. Later, I'll show you how to set alerts for when these markdowns occur, so you are one of the first to know.

When items are priced at 50% off, the light is *yellow*. Use caution. Sometimes you need to pass on the buying opportunity, other times you have just caught the tail end of the green light and it's a safe purchase. Toys that often pass the *yellow* test are Legos, Nerf Guns, and higher priced electronic toys. Many of the same reasons that you should not buy at 30% off still apply when the light is yellow. The main reason is that you want to buy at the lowest possible point, and you have advanced knowledge that the price will go lower. You just must be patient. I don't yell at people if they want to buy the bigger ticket or bigger brand name items at 50% off. Between resellers and deal hunting average customers, some of the really good stuff can get scooped up quickly. Sometimes it is necessary to buy at 50% if the item is right and it simply will not be on the shelf much longer.

When you see items that are 70% off, the light is almost always *green*. Buying at 70% off ensures that you are buying at the very bottom of the market. There may be others across the country that are buying the same item, but at least you know that they are not beating you on price, not even wholesalers. Sometimes you have to really do your research with the 70% off items because the market on Amazon is already reflecting all of the sellers that have jumped on the listing because they bought too soon at 30-50% off! This is when you really want to look at the historical data on the product before making a buying decision (I'll show you how to look at the historical data in Chapter 4).

Wal-Mart

Wal-Mart is my favorite store to source products from. Wal-Mart, like Target, typically does two major toy markdowns a year. The first is also right after Christmas in December and January, while the second typically starts in July, later than Target, and runs into early August. Wal-Mart, as you may have picked up on, is not as organized as Target in their mark-downs. Many of the toys that Wal-Mart puts on clearance are nationwide, but they also give much more freedom to individual stores. What does this mean? This means that some toys may be on clearance in one store, but the store across town doesn't have the same toy on clearance at all. Also, while Target's clearance prices typically are very closely aligned from store to store, Wal-Mart's prices may have considerable discrepancies between their stores. Nonetheless, Wal-Mart also follows a markdown schedule.

Wal-Mart typically likes to start their toy clearance at 25% off. The same logic for Target also applies here. Do *not* buy. Remember, the stop light is *red!* It will get marked down again, so do not buy in too early and miss out on better margins. When toys are 25% off, this is your time to scout the store and make lists of items you want to watch.

50% to 55% off is typically the next mark down. Again, this is an area in which you should use caution. I know that 50 to 55% off is a steal in most cases and that you risk missing out on certain items, but you'd be surprised at how many stores will further mark down items, especially at Wal-Mart. I'd rather miss out on some items and make a guaranteed profit on the items I am able to buy, rather than buy too early and forfeit all my margin to those that are able to buy lower.

Wal-Mart will discount items further than Target and usually end in the 75 to 80% off range. In rare cases, I've even seen 90% off. When you buy at 80% off and your competition buys at 50%, you hold all the leverage. I cannot stress the importance of buying at the bottom of the market when possible. Buying at bottom puts you in control and gives you a variety of options. You can sell sooner for a nice return or hold out for bigger profits.

Both Wal-Mart and Target will have additional clearances on toys throughout the year. At the time of this writing in Spring of 2019, there are several movies being released. *Marvel: End Game,*

Aladdin, and Detective Pikachu are some just to name a few. Since these movies all appeal to kids, Wal-Mart and Target must clear out more toys than they typically do this time of year to make room for all the new toys related to these movies. Cycles like this happen every year and you are able to build a Toyfolio year-round.

One thing that I have learned about Wal-Mart is that they give more freedom to individual department managers. Each department is given what they call "mark down money," at the beginning of each month. Essentially, this is a set budget where they have the liberty to mark down items in their department. This is one the main reasons you see such discrepancies various stores in prices for the exact same item.

Therefore, if you encounter a clearance item in a Wal-Mart store that you would like to purchase, it doesn't hurt to ask them if they will mark them down further if you agree to buy all of the item. Most people don't realize that you can negotiate with managers on price, but in many cases, you can! Yes, I have had managers look at me like I have three heads when I've asked for a discount. I have even had some laugh in my face. However, I have had others act like they are at their own yard sale and almost beg me to take stuff off the shelves for them!

First and foremost, ask for the toy department manager or the store manager. They are the only ones that will have authority to make a deal with you. Smile, shake their hand, and introduce yourself. Be as friendly as possible. The key question you want to ask them is, "do you have any more mark down money?" or "if I buy all of these items on clearance here, will you use some of your mark down money to give me a better deal?" Have a price point in mind and work your negotiation toward that number. If the sale price is not yet 70 to 80% off of the regular retail price, mention that you know the store will eventually mark the item down to that price. Simply ask if they would consider preemptively lowering the price to or near the eventual price *if* you agree to make shelf space for them. This is a WIN/WIN for both parties. Remember, they *want* their shelf space back. They need it to be able to bring in new inventory that they are required to carry. You are offering a solution to their problem and providing a valuable service to them!

Example

Now that you understand the common way most Amazon sellers operate versus the buy and hold strategy, as well as major store markdown schedules, let's look at a quick example using simple back of the envelope math to tie the two together before we talk about more places to find toys.

Toy A sells for $40 at most major retailers across the country. Since Amazon is not in stock, there is a small discrepancy in the market and the price has historically been $48 on Amazon. Target decides to no longer carry Toy A and puts it on clearance with a first markdown of 30% off. This brings the price down to $28 in Target. Most Amazon sellers will see this $20 disparity between $48 and $28 and jump on it to make a quick sale. After Amazon fees, they may stand to make an even $10 profit if the item is small and light enough.

What actually happens, is that hundreds of other Amazon sellers find the same deal and the price on Amazon stabilizes at the $38 range where most sellers are making pennies in profit. A couple weeks go by and Target marks Toy A down to 50% off ($20). The same cycle occurs all over again. Many more sellers jump on the listing because they can make $10 in profit in that $18 gap in price after all fees.

Before long, a couple short weeks after Target put Toy A on clearance, the price on Amazon has descended to $28. This is the price point at which those who bought the item for $20 are breaking even and even worse, those who bought it for $28 are in the red. Target then finishes their clearance cycle at 70% off, bringing Toy A to $12 in stores. If you are patient enough to wait to buy at $12, or even $20, then you control the market for the item.

Pretty soon, the price will stabilize as sellers sell out. In most instances, if it had a good Amazon best seller rank, this means that it at least returns to its historic price. In this example, that would be $48. Buying at $12 and selling at $48 after fees would possibly net you close to a 200% return on investment. The better the Amazon sales rank, the sooner the price will stabilize at a historic level that is profitable. The higher the sales rank, the longer period of time until the toy reaches profitable price point. If it has a lower sales rank, since it is no longer available in stores, the price on Amazon can often exceed the historical price of $48, because Amazon is the only place customers can find the item. This is why it is so important not to rush to sell an item as soon as you buy it. Instead, study the market, buy at a lower price than most sellers, and wait out everyone beating each other up on price, so that you can sell when you want at a margin you prefer.

Amazon

Yes, you can buy products from Amazon and resell them on Amazon. They are a retailer just like Wal-Mart and Target. The trick to a good Amazon to Amazon flip is to understand Keepa (I'll explain Keepa in the next chapter in depth). If you know that Amazon will go out of stock for a particular toy and that toy sells for more when they are out of stock, then you can buy from Amazon while they are in stock and resell it for more while Amazon is out of stock. The only rule to follow is that you cannot use an Amazon Prime account to purchase the items. You must order your items with a non-Prime buying account or with an Amazon business account.

Discount and Regional Stores

There are all kinds of stores across the country that pride themselves in being discount stores, such as TJ Maxx, Ross, Home Goods, Tuesday Morning, and Marshalls. These stores all have unique toy departments. What is special about these toy departments is that they, like the other items in the store, are overstock buys, older editions, clearance buys from other stores, etc.

Remember when I said in Chapter 2 that when major retailers clearance items that this typically means they are gone for good from retail shelves? This is where the other part of "typically" comes into the equation. While many toys will never be seen again in a retail store, others will find their way into various types of discount stores so that the store can have a toy department. It doesn't make sense for these types of stores to have relationships will toy brands and manufacturers to carry brand new toys at brand new toy prices. Customers shopping these stores want deals and carrying older toys allows them to give their customers those deals.

When assembling a Toyfolio, older toys are exactly what you want to find. In many cases, older toys have already increased in value. Finding them in discount stores a year or more after they have disappeared from the shelves of major retailers builds sizable margins. Plus, with older toys, you have the benefit of looking at historical data on the item and making a better buying decision. The catch with finding toys from these stores is that their supply is typically very low. They may only carry a maximum of ten of one particular toy, while two to three of one toy is the norm. The time to catch the best deals at these stores is right before Christmas.

Discount stores will beef up their toy department for the holiday season to make Christmas shopping for their customers easier and more convenient. During this time, you can find really great deals on high margin items. Just remember though, that the very nature of how these stores stock toys limits how much of the "good stuff" they will carry.

Regional stores are great places to build a Toyfolio. The main stores that come to my mind are Ollie's and Meijer. Ollie's is major discount store mainly located in the Southeast United States and Meijer is a major retailer on the level of Wal-Mart and Target, but primarily has retail locations in the Mid-West. Regional stores offer a great advantage when it comes to the buy and hold strategy and building a Toyfolio. That advantage is once again, *limited supply*. Buying toys that many people in the country cannot access, then you have a smaller number of sellers competing to sell the same high demand item, which puts more profit in your pockets.

I cannot speak to Meijer, as I do not live in the Mid-West, but I do have access to Ollie's. Ollie's prides itself on being a low-budget, discount retailer that has limited time deals, which are dependent upon the many liquidation buys it makes from various retailers and manufacturers throughout the year. If you walk through their stores, you'll most likely hear a recording say, "Get up to 70% off the fancy stores' prices, but you gotta act fast, because once they're gone, they're gone!" Ollie's, like many stores, increases their supply of toys as the holidays approach. I tend to start scouting out toys there in late summer. Once you know what you are looking at and can read historical data on toys, you'll be able to spot some real gems in there during the late summer that simply will not be available any longer as Christmas approaches. After the late summer acquisition, they will once again expand their toy selection heavily in October and November. By December, many items have been picked over, but you can still find some great diamonds in the rough. Sign up for the Ollie's Army Rewards if you have one in your area. It's not a credit card, but rather a rewards card. You'll get 10% coupons in the mail and you'll be invited to Ollie's night in mid-December, when all toys are 25% off. In all likelihood, you won't be able to sell any of them before Christmas, but it'll be a great start to the Toyfolio you'll be building for the coming year.

Rural Stores

There are pros and cons to sourcing products in both big cities and rural areas. Large cities have more stores from which you can source, but the deals are typically scooped up faster. Rural areas have fewer stores from which you can choose, but deals are typically more widely available. In my experience, rural stores usually outperform more metropolitan stores. This has a lot to do with population, competition, and mismanaged stores.

For example, the county in which I live had just under 23,000 people at the last 2017 census. The largest town in in this county has just over 5,000 people living within the town limits. This town is home to the only Wal-Mart in the county. We don't even have a Target or a Starbucks! Gasp, I know. Many people would call it the end of the earth; I call it home.

In stark contrast, Raleigh, NC is only an hour and half away from where I live. At the time of 2017 census, Raleigh had a population of roughly 465,000 in the city limits and all of Wake County was home to almost 1.1 million people. The city of Raleigh has 6 Wal-Mart Supercenters and as a whole, Wake County has 13.

Now let's do some back of the envelope math using the Snow Glow Elsa that was the hot toy everyone was chasing when I first started. Let's say that Wal-Mart sends 100 units of this toy to every Wal-Mart store in the country. That seems fair and easy, right? While it makes things easy for Wal-Mart, it creates opportunities for us.

In all of Wake County, there would be 1,300 Snow Glow Elsa's available between the 13 Wal-Mart stores. If all the 1.1 million people wanted a Snow Glow Elsa, they would have a 0.0012 chance of obtaining one. In contrast, while only 100 Snow Glow Elsa's would be available in my county, since there are only 23,000 people, everyone would have a 0.0043 chance of securing one. Thus, Wake county has 13 times more toys than my county, but residents in my county have over a 3.5 times greater chance of finding a Snow Glow Elsa.

Obviously, everyone in the county doesn't want one of these toys, but if you then factor in the average age of the residents, you may see even more discrepancies with buying toys. The average person in my county is much older than the average resident of Wake County. Younger populations have more kids; thus, they buy more toys than those in my county.

Another factor is simply socio-economic status. On average, a family in Wake County has more discretionary spending money than a family from my county. This results in more profitable inventory being left on the shelves in my county.

Therefore, if you live in a rural area, embrace it! While your initial thought may be that you can't do this because you have fewer stores, you are at an advantage in many ways. If you live in a more metropolitan area, in many ways it can be to your advantage to venture outside of the city. One rural store can have more valuable inventory than many of the city stores combined.

Brickseek

When I started selling on Amazon, what I would find from store to store was very hit or miss. If I found a great clearance toy at Wal-Mart, sometimes I would find it at other Wal-Mart stores and other times, I didn't. It could be very frustrating and rewarding at the same time because I was walking into stores completely blind, not knowing what I would find. The thrill of the hunt kept me motivated to go to more stores even when I struck out.

Then, I joined a BOLO (Be on the lookout) Facebook group in which a small group of sellers from around the country shared profitable items that they were finding in real time. This group was great because it opened my eyes to products I had been missing and gave me a list of what to look for in stores.

One day in this group, someone posted a great BOLO, but he concluded his post by stating that we could check brickseek.com to see if an item was available in our area. Excuse me? Come again? You mean that I can check a website that will tell me where to find profitable items!? Better yet, in some cases, it'll tell me how many they have!? No way! I was very skeptical. The item he had posted was $7 at Wal-Mart and was selling very well on Amazon for $40. I looked up the item on Brickseek and it said that only one store in my area had them. Early the next morning, I went shopping. I went to the store and low and behold, the store had the exact number in stock that Brickseek said it did. I walked out of there with seven of the items, which yielded over $150 in profit. That is another day I will never forget. It was like the Halloween night when I first learned about selling on Amazon. Once I learned about Brickseek.com, it forever changed how I run my Amazon business and build my Toyfolio year after year.

Essentially, Brickseek is website that is synched with many of the largest retailers in the country. At the time of this writing, Brickseek tracks in store inventory at Wal-Mart, Target, Lowes, Office Depot, CVS, Home Depot, Staples, Macys and BJs. Brickseek also tracks online deals at Wal-Mart, Target, Amazon, Best Buy, Macys, and Tiger Direct. I don't know all the technicalities of how it does this; I just know that it is magical!

Now instead of blindly walking into stores, I know what I am looking for and how many items there should be. Brickseek is like x-ray glasses that allow you to save time and energy by only going to stores in your area that have profitable items in stock. If you are living in a city and I've convinced you to venture out into the country to find a rural store, you can now know if it is worth your time before you ever get in the car! Let's look at an example:

Walmart Supercenter #3864 561 Yopp Rd Jacksonville NC 28540 (771 Miles Away) Google Maps / Apple Maps	Limited Stock	$17.00 43% off	⊕ Shopping List
Walmart Supercenter #7179 1109 W Corbett Ave Swansboro NC 28584 (775 Miles Away) Google Maps / Apple Maps	Out of Stock	$7.00 77% off	⊕ Shopping List
Walmart Supercenter #2000 5400 N Croatan Hwy Ste 100 Kitty Hawk NC 27949 (75 Miles Away) Google Maps / Apple Maps	In Stock Quantity: 64	$7.00 77% off	⊕ Shopping List

In the picture above, we are looking at inventory levels and prices for a board game that Walmart had on clearance. As you can see, one store says that it has "limited stock." In my experience, this means that they possibly have one or two left. You'll also notice that they are on their second markdown phase as their price is at $17. The other two stores shown are on their final markdown at $7 with one store out of stock and the other showing in stock. Just like that, with a few clicks, I can see which stores are worth my time and which are not.

As of this writing, Brickseek recently changed the format in which they report Walmart inventory levels. Hopefully, it will change back to the old format that shows you an exact number, but for now, if they have 7 or if they have 77, the number displayed on Brickseek will only display 6+. Annoying, but it is what it is. I typically go after large quantities of items in stock, so this simple change is definitely going to affect my business going forward. Nonetheless, having a tool to tell you which stores are in stock versus which stores are out of stock, revolutionizes how we can shop for profitable inventory.

Speaking of changes, Brickseek has recently (Q4 2018) undergone some major modifications. Back when I first started using it, it was simply a website where you could look and see if stores around you had items you had already found in another store or of which you had previous knowledge. You would simply enter the item's UPC and run results for your zip code. After the many changes that they've made, you can use their website to find profitable items that you have never seen in store before. Better yet, they now have a feature where you can find tons of profitable items that are available online.

When I first began using Brickseek, it was completely free. They now have 3 different plans available for those that want to use their site. The first plan is still free, and you can make a living finding products using their free service. Their premium version is $9.99/month and gives you many additional features. Their extreme deal hunter package runs $29.99/month and gives access to every feature the site has.

I know everyone has various budgets and to some $29.99/month seems steep. I do not get paid to endorse Brickseek at all, but let me tell you from experience that it is worth every penny. On days when I follow a lead from Brickseek,

I may go to as many as 15 stores in a day looking for the items. Many times, the profit that I make from just the first store more than pays for *months* of Brickseek's subscription plan; and that is just *one* store on *one* day. If you are following the guidance in this book and hit clearance in January or July, you'll pay for an entire year's subscription within a week. I have profited tens of thousands of dollars in just the few short years I have used the service. It's worth the $29.99 a month. However, try the free version for a few months before you are ready to pay for a subscription, especially if you are new to selling toys.

That being said, I don't want to only talk about how great Brickseek is, I want to show you in person. I want to give you an in depth look at Brickseek. Before you spend a dime on a Brickseek subscription, watch the videos I have created that show you the difference in the plans they offer. The videos can be found in the Toyfolio Facebook group I've created for all Toyfolio training videos. It's completely free, so just ask to join the group, watch the videos in which you are interested, then go apply what you've learned. Better yet, if you have a question, you can ask me through the group, and I'll do my best to get back with you as soon as possible. Just search "Toyfolio" on Facebook and you should be able to find it. If not, join the Facebook group here:

https://www.facebook.com/groups/420743422184393/

Getting Ungated

"Gated," and "ungated," are definitely Amazon words that bring about joy or frustration. Gated means that you do not have permission to sell a certain product, brand, or anything in a particular category. Ungated means that you are free to sell it. Obviously, this is exclusive to Amazon. You can sell just about anything in accordance with the law on any other platform without restrictions. However, Amazon plays by different rules. Remember how we talked about the fact that people trust Amazon to get them the right product? To some degree, this is how they do it. While some products are still counterfeited and there are rogue sellers that do not obey Amazon's rules, the ungating process is Amazon's way of vetting sellers to assure that they are selling authentic products.

Back in the day when FBA was first introduced, it was more of the Wild, Wild West. Anything could be sold, and sellers had a lot of freedom. Everyone was automatically free to sell in most categories. If you were gated in a category, then all you had to do was submit retail receipts to prove authenticity and become ungated. I did this immediately when I opened my account. The grocery category was originally gated. I submitted a receipt with grocery related items and was instantly approved. That explains my first sale of red velvet pancake mix.

Most, but not all, of the good toy brands that you will want to sell are gated to new sellers. Obviously, this creates an issue, as, you cannot build a Toyfolio without toys. Thankfully, the solution is simple.

Amazon no longer accepts retail receipts as documentation to qualify to be ungated. They now require invoices from authorized distributors *or* a direct letter from the manufacturer to be approved. Unless you have a personal connection, sometimes those letters can be very hard to come by. Luckily, we can easily use authorized distributors. These are wholesalers that sell officially licensed and branded products to resellers like us and other retail stores.

Amazon likes to see an order of at least 10 of an item on the invoice in order to be approved. I don't know why this is, I just know that 10 is the magic number. Do not get paralysis by analysis when buying an item to start the ungating process. Sure, ideally, we want to buy an item that will make us a profit. However, the ultimate goal is to get ungated in a specific brand. For example, the Barbie brand will make you thousands in your lifetime. Find a small profit or break-even item to order from the distributor to use to get ungated. However, I would argue that if you wait to find the perfect item from the distributor, you will lose money in opportunity costs because you won't be able to capitalize on deals at retail stores and websites.

Most people that go through this process find the cheapest thing that they can possibly find from a certain brand. They can buy 10 $3 Barbie keychains and that suffices as enough to get ungated. $30 spent to be approved to sell that brand is money well spent.

Listed below are two of the most popular distributors that sellers use to get ungated. In order to apply for an account, you'll need to have a federal tax ID or your state issued sales tax number. I know this sounds intimidating and like a daunting task. Do not stop here out of fear. You can easily get both in a matter of hours from the IRS website as well as your state's department of revenue site. Once you have these, simply apply for an account, order, submit invoices to Amazon, and then start building your Toyfolio. The two distributors are:

Entertainment Earth:

https://www.entertainmentearth.com

Shepher:

https://www.shepher.com

4
HOW DO I KNOW WHICH TOYS TO BUY?

If you haven't been paying close attention yet, this is where I really need you to focus. If you "get," this chapter, you will be well on your way to building a highly profitable Toyfolio.

Buying the right inventory and passing on the wrong inventory is a science. I've been selling on Amazon and eBay long enough to see many people post "deals" to various BOLO groups that quite honestly are terrible purchases. It breaks my heart seeing people sink money into bad inventory and knowing that they are going to be sitting on that inventory for a long, long time without many ever selling. I wish I had the time to walk every single one of them through *why* that purchase, or deal isn't quite such a deal. Doing so would take up too much time on an individual basis, which is why I am writing this book.

The first thing you must understand is that there is a massive difference between *list* price and *selling* price. Just because an item is listed for a certain price does not mean that it is actually selling for that price. So many people do not understand this concept. Consequently, this is why you see "articles," posted in your newsfeed about how a certain Beanie Baby is "selling," for $100,000 on eBay. Then, you see 300 people comment saying that they have that exact one and how excited they are to become aware of such a windfall. Most likely, that Beanie Baby isn't selling for $100,000; someone has it listed for $100,000. Plus, if 300 people instantly comment on the post saying that they have the exact one, this means that there is obviously way more supply out there than anyone realized. And you know that if there is a surplus of supply and demand is low (when was the last time you went Beanie Baby hunting?), then that is going to be reflected in price. So, you may get $10 for that Beanie Baby on eBay if particular person has to have right then, but I'd be willing to bet that a sale price of 10 cents at a yard sale is a safer bet.

On eBay, you can filter search results by *Sold* items. This feature gives you exact data as to what an item actually sold for and when it sold. If you look at the time stamp on the listing and multiples of the same item have sold in a given day, then you have a hot item. If the time stamp on one listing is from Tuesday, but the next sold item is from 8 months ago, then you have something that isn't selling that well, is very rare, or only sells when it is available for sale. Something cannot sell if it isn't available for sale.

Amazon does not have a feature like eBay where you can look up sold items by a particular seller. However, based on Amazon's best sellers rank and a few other tools, we can see the price at which something sold in the past and we can get a very close estimate as to the pace at which an item is selling in amount of particular time.

Keepa

When I was first starting my Amazon journey, like I've said before, I was selling items as soon as I could find them. I participated in the race to the bottom and likely shorted myself thousands of dollars. I was not paying attention to Keepa or Brickseek at all that year. Nonetheless, I still put $12k in my pocket on a very limited part-time basis. Since that first year, simply understanding Keepa and Brickseek has allowed me to make 4x that amount in virtually the same amount of time. So, what in the world is Keepa?

Keepa.com is a website, as well as a Google Chrome extension, that tracks virtually every item on Amazon. When I say track, I mean they *track everything* related to specific items on Amazon. They track price history for FBA and FBM items for new, used, and collectible conditions, the number of offers/sellers, how often Amazon has been in and out of stock, and Amazon's best sellers rank. Thus, if you understand the Keepa chart for a particular item, you know more than the average seller and can make the best possible informed buying decision.

I rarely make a buying decision without first looking at a Keepa chart. If you are just using your Amazon seller app or another third-party scanning app to scan items in store, then you are missing out on vital information that will help you make better buying decisions. The Amazon seller app is like having tunnel vision that only shows you what is happening with an item at that moment. Keepa allows you to see all the historical data for that item, giving you a bigger picture to make a decision. You can access the Keepa website on your smartphone, but some scanning apps have direct links that can take you straight to the product page without having to type in everything. I use Scoutify, the app that comes from being an Inventory Lab (more on Inventory Lab later) user. I have also heard good things about the Legendary sourcing app but have never used it personally.

I hate saying that a paid tool is essential, but in my opinion, I cannot implement the Buy and Hold strategy without Keepa. It's just one of those things that makes me more money than it costs me. At the time of writing this first edition, Keepa has just started charging for their services. For years, everything was free, but in the beginning of 2019, another price tracking service called Camel Camel Camel went down. When this service crashed, they lost all the historical data for items they were tracking on Amazon. Thus, when this happened, Keepa found themselves with a monopoly on historical Amazon data. Luckily, they do not charge out the nose for their services. Currently (November 2019), you can get access to all of their features and data for $17 per month or $117 per year. It is worth every penny and my business simply cannot run without it. Camel Camel Camel is also back up and running, by the way. It is free if you choose to use it. I personally prefer and recommend Keepa. Here is an example of what Keepa looks like:

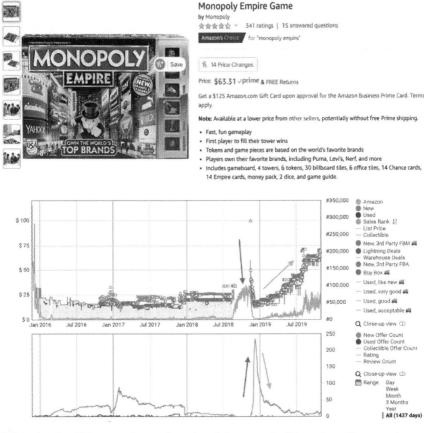

This is the Keepa chart for the Monopoly Empire Game. A lot is going on here, so let's break it down:

- The orange shaded area represents when Amazon is in stock. We can see from the top portion of the graph that Amazon ran out of stock during the summer of 2018 and has not been in stock since.

- The blue line in the bottom portion of the graph represents the number of offers. This line indicates how many sellers are selling this particular item at a given point in time. It shifts up as sellers come onto the listing and down as they sell out.

- The green squiggly line that looks like a seismograph is the Amazon best sellers rank marker. The tighter the line, the faster it is selling. The looser and wider spread the drops in the graph are, the slower the item is selling.

- Blue squares represent sellers that are selling the item FBM.

- Red triangles represent sellers that are selling the item FBA.

- Pink diamonds represent the buy box. The buy box is the price and seller that Amazon awards when a customer comes to buy the item.

You can turn on or off many of these features on the right-hand side of the graph simply by clicking on the various features.

Now, for the story on this toy and graph. Amazon was in stock for three years and averaged a price of approximately $20, until they sold out during the summer of 2018. At that point, there were no other sellers, so the bottom graph went to zero. Consequently, the green sales rank graph started to trend upward. After all, the sales rank isn't going to improve when there are no items to sell. Suddenly, there was a rush of sellers that peaked at 235 sellers, as seen on the bottom graph. Why did this happen? Because one of the first sellers to the listing had it and sold the toy for $50. Did I mention that you could find these toys for $5 at Five Below stores and on their website? What you had in this situation was a cheap and widely available item selling for 10x the amount on Amazon. Those 235 sellers flooded the market, as indicated by the red, upward pointing arrow on the graph. As a result, the price plummeted below $14.50, at which point, people were making pennies. This is also indicated on the graph by the red, downward facing arrow in the top half of the chart. The green arrows show how the number of sellers decreased as they sold out and consequently, the price rose. This is a perfect example of when to sell and when not to sell. As you look at the number of sellers' data, there you will notice that it makes the shape of a mountain. The mountain's peak is typically when the price reflected on Amazon is at its lowest. This is not the time to sell. As we build a Toyfolio, we always want to wait to sell at the point at which the side of the mountain bottoms out on the right side. This is where the price normalizes to the price it was before there was an influx of sellers or exceeds that price. In this case, the price skyrocketed. It's a fun place to be when you are sitting on a pile of inventory and the price does that.

Again, if you hop over to the Toyfolio Facebook group, then you can see all kinds of free training videos on Keepa. Obviously, I cannot make you go watch these videos. This book is simply an introduction to the concept of a Toyfolio. The real meat that will change your business can be found in these free videos. It's simply much easier to show you in a video that to try to write it all out here. Go watch the videos and if you have any questions, you can ask anything there in the group. That's also the advantage to watching the videos; you get to directly ask me anything you don't understand and I'll do my best to walk you through it.

Here's the link again:

https://www.facebook.com/groups/420743422184393/

5

WHERE DO I STORE INVENTORY AND HOW DO I KNOW WHEN TO SELL?

My wife and I live in a 1,000 square foot house. We have one bathroom and you can stand at the entrance of it and see into every room in the house. It's close quarters. Much to my wife's displeasure, I operated out of the living room for first two years as an Amazon seller.

In the fall of 2016, we completed a detached garage that is almost as big as our house and our marriage was saved. It is 24 feet by 36 feet. The front 24' x 24' of the garage was suppose be just that, a traditional garage. The back portion (12 feet by 24 feet), would be my Amazon lair.

Long story short, we have never parked a car in our garage. Oops. It has a few garage-esque things in it like garden tools and such, but it essentially has been overrun with my Amazon business. Storing items there saves me thousands in Amazon storage fees, especially since I hold inventory for such a long period of time. This storage leverage that I have is another vital piece to the buy and hold strategy. I am able to wait out other sellers to sell out of a product because I am able to store the items myself for free.

Amazon FBA is a magical program. I cannot say enough good

about it, but it does have a fee structure when it comes to inventory storage. Remember all those people that buy inventory and send it in immediately and race to the bottom to get a sale? Once their inventory hits Amazon warehouses, the clock starts ticking on how long they have before they start incurring monthly storage fees and long-term storage fees.

Amazon does not like it when inventory arrives at their fulfillment centers and just sits. Those places are meant to hum with efficiency and move products to billions of customers worldwide every day. They are not interested in having your stuff just sit there and not sell. If that's what you choose to do with your inventory, then Amazon gladly charges you for the opportunity.

Thus, your competition in many cases is being pressured to sell from two sides. One, many people are buying their inventory on credit and need it to sell within a month to pay off their balance. Two, many people are in a rush to sell because Amazon is constantly reminding sellers to sell inventory that is just sitting around. Amazon sends emails and gives you notifications in your account to move slow selling inventory.

Most recently, within the past year or two, Amazon has introduced what they call their IPI score, or Inventory Performance Index score. This score is determined by an algorithm that grades you on how well your inventory is doing. Have inventory just sitting around and not selling? This is bad and drives your score down. Score too low? Amazon then reserves the right to dictate how much product you can send in in the future. Talk about pressure to sell!

Therefore, storage is big issue when it comes to Buy and Hold. You need to figure out where you want to store your products. Have a spare bedroom? Garage? I know people who rent out storage units year-round to implement the buy and hold strategy. Storage units are far cheaper than paying Amazon storage fees. Enduring the small inconvenience of having products in your house or a storage unit will yield thousands of dollars over time.

Or build a garage…you know, so you can park your car in it one day.

The point is to think just a little differently than your competition. Even if you can hold inventory for a minimum of a month before sending it into the Amazon fulfillment centers, you are one month ahead in storage fees over your competition. This affords you more time to sell at a higher price point after others have sold out.

Knowing when to send in

I've been asked how I know when to send in inventory countless times over the last couple years. The short answer is, it depends on the specific item. This is another topic that is better explained in the Keepa videos on the Toyfolio Facebook page. Keepa tells you everything you need to know as far as when it is a good time to sell, if you can read the graph correctly. You can also get Keepa to send you alerts when an item reaches your desired selling price. Again, I'll show you in the videos how that all works. Toyfolio Facebook page. Go there.

Being efficient

I also get asked how I prep/store my inventory year-round. After all, buying and holding items lends itself to becoming overwhelmed and swamped with inventory piling up all around you. It doesn't have to be this way. It is possible to stay completely organized and on top of your inventory.

First of all, I like to go ahead and list my inventory and leave it as inactive. For those of you who are new, inactive simply means that it is not available for sale, but the product exists in your Amazon inventory. You can do these one of two ways. One, through SellerCentral (Amazon's seller portal where each seller controls their selling account) or two, through Inventory Lab (a third-party service that synchs with SellerCentral).

Personally, I prefer Inventory Lab. It's much smoother, cleaner, and has additional features that make my life easier. For one, I can enter all my purchase data into Inventory Lab when creating a new listing. This information includes the quantity, the store from which I purchased the inventory, the buy cost, and the date. Inventory Lab can then spit out profit and loss reports based on your sales data and special reports to show you which stores are your most profitable. Cool stuff. Amazon itself does not have these features.

Once I enter all this vital information into Inventory Lab, they will tell me if the item needs any special prep such as being poly bagged or bubble wrapped. From here, I can also choose to send the products feeds (Inventory Lab jargon for product data) to my Seller Central account without creating a shipment. For those familiar with Amazon, make sure you catch that. I am sending product feeds without creating shipments. Amazon does not like when shipments are created and then deleted or not sent. Sending product feeds without creating shipments simply populates the product listings in my inactive inventory.

From here, I can go ahead and prep my items since Inventory Lab already told me how they needed to be prepped. I can even go ahead and box items of the same SKU together and have the box ready to be shipped at a moment's notice months from now. Buy how do I know where Amazon will send my items? How can I go ahead and box items up ready to be sent into FBA?

Good question. Glad you asked. At this time, Amazon likes to send like products of the same SKU to redistribution fulfillment centers. From there, if they have enough of a similar item, they can split up and send them to the fulfillment centers of their choice. The magic number for this is 18. In my experience and that of many other sellers, if you have at least 18 of one item, then Amazon will assign you one warehouse to which you will ship your inventory. Send in 17 or less of the same item and Amazon is going to put the logistical burden on you. They will split 17 items into 4 or 5 shipments and make you send 4 or 5 boxes to 4 or 5 different fulfillment centers. This could be one in California, one in Texas, one in Pennsylvania, and so on. However, if I send 18, then for me it all goes to Charlotte, in my home state.

This has huge ramifications for your business efficiency. Sending everything to one warehouse saves a ton of time and allows you to prep the items months ahead of time, not to mention the shipping costs it saves. With working a full-time job around my part-time Amazon job, time is very valuable to me. Sending out shipments is no easy task in the middle of a busy week. Peace of mind is knowing that I have several products that are ready to go and I could complete a shipment in a matter of about 10 minutes if I needed to get a shipment out that day. I simply have to enter box dimensions and weights into Seller Central and my shipment is out the door.

Toyfolio by Greg Webb

6
WHAT WILL I NEED AND
WHAT IS THE COST TO GET STARTED?

Here is a list of the items you need to run a Toyfolio business:

1. Computer – you're reading an e-commerce business book in 2019…chances are, you have one.

2. Printer – if you don't have one, you can get started with a cheaper $30-50 one.

3. Smartphone – if you're still using a flip phone, close this book and contact me for a refund. ☺

4. Cardboard boxes for shipping – you can get used boxes for free at many stores if you ask the manager. Otherwise, they'll run you $1.50 to $2 at Wal-Mart or Lowes.

5. Tape and Tape Dispenser

6. Digital Scale

7. Somewhere to store products – I operate out of my garage. Maybe you have a garage as well or perhaps a spare bedroom or office. Maybe a family member has room in their basement. Worst case scenario is to rent out a storage unit. If you're implementing the buy and hold strategy,

you'll save yourself money renting out a storage unit rather than paying Amazon storage fees.

8. Item labels — Amazon requires you to label items with their unique barcode. You can get these at most any superstore or office supply store, as well as anywhere online.

9. Poly-bags — Amazon requires that some toys be poly-bagged, such as plush stuffed animals. Just make sure that they have a suffocation warning on them, per Amazon policy. You can get these on Amazon.com, Uline.com, or a variety of other sites.

Here is a list of the services you'll need to use and/or pay for monthly:

1. **Amazon seller account**. Amazon has two seller account plans. This first is called an individual selling account. This account is free. When you sell an item, Amazon will deduct their fees from the sale price of the item and charge you $1 for each item you sell.

   The Amazon professional selling account is $39.99 a month. Amazon deducts fees from the sale price of every item you sell but does not charge a $1 per item fee. Therefore, if you're selling over 40 items per month, then it makes sense to have a professional selling account. This fee was big hang up for me when I first opened my account, but I have not noticed it since I began. Amazon deducts it from your account balance automatically and I have sold at least 40 items per month since I began.

2. **Insurance**. It stinks, but it's part of life and it's part of Amazon's terms of service if you have a professional selling account. You can sell items on other online platforms and not be required to carry insurance, but it's not very wise. People sue over anything these days, so please protect yourself. If you're just starting out and only selling toys you find in retail stores on Amazon, a general

liability policy at the time of this edition will run you roughly $500 a year and that covers up to a million dollars in coverage. Don't let less than $42 a month keep you from protecting yourself and your family.

3. **Brickseek**. I've already talked extensively about Brickseek. I recommend eventually getting the $29.99/month subscription, but use the free version when you first start. Put some money in the bank and prove to yourself that it works and then get the $29.99 plan.

4. **Keepa**. This is another site that I have already talked about at length. I honestly cannot build a Toyfolio using the Buy and Hold strategy without Keepa. It makes me way more money than it costs me. Save money by buying the yearly subscription at $117/year in advance or break it down to $17/ month. Again, use the free version until you get the hang of it. The free version will get you started, but you will not have access to all of the information Keepa provides to make the best buying decisions.

5. **Inventory Lab**. There is no shortage of Amazon tools and subscription services. If you aren't careful, they can really eat into your profits. Inventory Lab is a luxury and not a necessity for those starting out. I went two years without subscribing, but after using it for a number of years, I wish I had started using it sooner. Inventory Lab is a service that allows you to list and manage all of your inventory on Amazon. I find listing and shipping inventory with Inventory Lab much easier than using my seller account. My favorite feature is their accounting software that allows you to enter cost of goods sold while listing.

6. **Sales tax services**. Sales tax is intimidating. I know. However, it is one of those necessary evils you must deal with if you are going to build a legitimate business online. *Do not* let this one thing keep you from starting. While it is scary to most, there are ways to manage sales tax

without pulling out your hair. I use a service called Tax Jar and they sync their services with my Amazon account. They tell me how much I've collected and how much needs to go where. It's all handled for you. Their services start around $20 per month.

At the time of this first edition, within the last several months, Amazon has taken the burden of sales tax collection out of third-party seller's hands for many states. This means that they handle it for you and you can sleep easily at night. Amazon collects for some and not others. Since late 2018 and on a monthly basis, Amazon seems to be adding new states for which they collect taxes. At the very least, you will need to register in your home state. Your state issued sales tax ID number is the number you need to open wholesale accounts and to get ungated. Again, do not let this keep you from starting. Start your business, prove to yourself that it works, then start figuring out these kinds of things.

The nice thing about filing state sales tax returns (if there is such a positive), is that your state issued sales tax ID number allows you to purchase items in stores tax free. Not every retailer does this, but Walmart, in particular, is very reseller friendly and gives you a card to present at checkout. You can also submit your information to buy tax free from Wal-Mart for any online purchases as well.

What if I have little to no money?

I talk about selling red velvet pancake mix and Batman belts when I first started, but I also sold used books and used toys to build capital. You can get used books and toys at thrift stores, estates sales, garage sales, Facebook marketplace, Craigslist, and more. In fact, you can resell this book in used condition after you finish and recoup some of your costs if you wish. I like resellers. ☺

The point is, there is opportunity everywhere. In fact, you could build your entire Toyfolio off of used items. You can find toy gold all over the place. Older used toys demand huge premiums because they embody everything we have discussed thus far in regard to supply and demand. Used, missing pieces, and broken toys can fetch crazy prices on sites like eBay because they are one of a kind.

A good friend of mine just last year found all of his old Star Wars and G.I. Joe toys from his childhood in the 1980s. All of them had endured their fair share of being played with. None of them were in original packaging, yet he sold them all on eBay for over $700!

You just have to get creative. You must hustle some and hunt through the thousands of deals that exist out there. You can get some serious capital if you put your nose to the ground and search for the inventory that will catapult your Toyfolio.

The best place to start is in your own house! Look around at everything you don't need, then sell it and get some capital in your pocket with which you can work.

Do you literally have zero money? Stalk the free section on craigslist and flip inventory that you get for free! Or, offer your selling services to people you know. There are people everywhere that have unwanted stuff in their house that they wish they could turn into cash. Their only problem? They don't have time or they don't know how. Make an ad offering to sell people's stuff for them for a commission, and you'll be surprised how much business you'll have.

What if I live outside the United States or I'm limited by time?

This isn't an excuse when it comes to building a Toyfolio. Yes, in many cases you will not be able to participate in the retail arbitrage deals available in the stores across the US, but you can purchase items online and send them into the US to sell on the US Amazon site.

One service that makes this scenario possible is a prep center. Prep centers are third party warehouses that receive your online orders for you instead of having products shipped to your house. These centers have limited access to your Amazon account, which limits them to only being able to create and send shipments for you. Thus, it really is as simple as buying an item online and having it shipped to a prep center. When the prep center receives it, the prep center prepares your shipment, then sends it to Amazon fulfillment centers for you, and you sell the items. Amazon sends you money and you never had to see or touch a product.

Prep centers do charge a fee to store and prep your inventory. Typically, it is approximately $1 per item, but the fees vary from place to place. If you are implementing more of the Buy and Hold strategy, these centers will also vary in longer term storage costs.

I do not personally use a prep center, but below are a few reputable prep centers that have been vetted by many in the Amazon selling community. There are dozens more that offer similar services. Many states have them and some are located in states with no sales tax, which is a nice bonus. Do your own research if this is an avenue you choose to explore. Prep centers are also the perfect solution for those that are limited by space and time.

- Pro Prep and Fulfillment

(proprepandfulfillment.com)

- Proven Prep Midwest

(provenprepmidwest.com)

- Australia Proprep & Fulfillment

(proprepandfulfillment.com.au/)

Something to seriously ask yourself

I realize that this seems like information overload and that all these subscriptions and expenses sound costly. When you've yet to sell an item, it's hard to imagine having to pay for all these things. That's why I recommend you use the free versions until you can get your feet wet. On the other hand, ask yourself where else in the world can you start a business and leverage the world's largest customer base for less than $100 a month?

Toyfolio by Greg Webb

7
BUY AND HOLD GOLD

The buy and hold strategy can be outrageously profitable with a number of toys from year to year. However, one line of toys stands above the rest – Legos.

I don't claim to be an expert in Legos. In fact, I know some people that know far more than I do about these little bricks. However, I do know that Legos are in a league of their own when it comes to resale value. I'd even venture to say they are close to being a currency of their own. The very nature of how Lego operates is the equivalent of setting a baseball on a tee for Babe Ruth; homeruns every time.

Lego produces sets based upon certain themes. Most themes center around popular movies that are being released during that particular year. These sets stay on store shelves for an average of 2 years, then they are eventually "retired," as Lego likes to call it. When these sets retire, they are never made again. Did you catch that? Never. Made. Again. This, like most items in the Buy and Hold strategy, boils down to simple economics. An item that is wildly popular that is never made again will, in most cases, only increase in value over time.

Legos are often the one exception to many toy sales that you will see in stores and online over the course of the year. In particular, Target runs multiple toy sales a year, yet in the fine print you'll frequently see that Legos are excluded. This is simply because they hold and retain their value so well. Plus, they are always in demand at retail prices, so why would a retailer want to lose that profit margin?

Typically, the only time that you will see Legos marked down in stores is in the clearance cycles in January and July that I talked about in Chapter 3. Other smaller clearances occur throughout the year from time to time as well. During these times, you will see Wal-Mart and Target both eventually mark down their Lego prices to 70 to 75% off of the retail price. I catch some flack every year for saying that, but it's true, and I find those deals every year.

This is where the highly populated cities versus rural areas come into play. While I can see Legos get to 70 to 75% off in rural areas around me, others in more populated areas rarely see them get to 50% off. In many cases, people grab them when they are first marked down to 25 to 30% off. Obviously, Wal-Mart is going to be the place the find the best deals because of this situation. I have a Wal-Mart in my town of 5,000 people, but Target simply does not put stores in markets that small. I have rarely caught Legos marked down for more than 50% off at Target because their stores are located in more populated areas. A higher population equals more competition.

In total, when Legos are marked down in January and July, you typically only have a 2 to 3-week window to capitalize on this opportunity. In some areas, the window may only be a few days. If you aren't paying attention by walking around stores and not utilizing Brickseek, then in many cases, you will miss it. I prefer the January markdown over the July markdown. The main reason is that many times when Legos hit at least 50% off, it is often times a few weeks removed from Christmas day. Parents and grandparents just spent hundreds, if not thousands, on gifts for their entire families, many of them being toys for their kids and grandkids. The last place they are 2 to 3 weeks after Christmas day, is in the toy section of a retail store. While some deal hunting parents will take advantage of this sale in January, many more will find the deals in July/August. In July or August, it's easier for a parent to see buying a great clearance Lego set with the intent to gift it in December, rather than doing the same thing in January. Below is a picture of two carts that I filled at 50% off this past January.

If you can exercise enough patience and delay gratification, Legos that you buy during these clearance cycles will yield tremendous returns long-term, as the supply for them dwindles and the demand for them stays steady.

The main thing I like about Legos is that when you buy them at 50% off or greater, you most always have multiple options when it comes to your exit strategy. Prices on Legos do tank on

Amazon after they go on clearance in retail stores in January and July, but it is very short lived. While some products can take a year to recover to their normal retail price on Amazon after third party sellers come on and tank the price, Legos almost always recover within a month or two. Some never go down in price at all. There is so much demand that even with a temporary surplus of supply, the price remains steady. This allows you to either hold the item for a short time and quickly make a profit, or you can hold long-term and make even more when the demand surges at Christmas, or better yet, once the set retires.

How do you know when a Lego set will retire? No one does, except Lego, until it happens. I have found the site retiringsets.com helpful in the past, but even then, this site is more of a conversation forum that gets you looking in the direction of the sets to which you should be paying attention.

Ultimately, retirement varies depending on the particular set, its popularity, and theme. In general terms, a new Lego set will land on retail shelves and stay there on average for one and half to two years. At this point, they will be marked down and cleared out never to be seen again in a retail store. While it may never be carried in stores any longer, retailers such as Walmart, Target, and Amazon may continue to carry it on their websites. This can continue for a year to a year and half. All in all, I have observed that on average, the retail life span of most Lego sets is three years. Sometimes, it may be two years, other times it's four. Thus, without looking at the specifics of a particular set, you can expect that if you buy Legos on clearance during the specified clearance seasons, you have an average of a year and a half before the set is no longer available anywhere at the original retail price. Once the set is no longer available at retail price and is retired, that is when the magic happens. Just to have some fun, let's look at a few examples from over the years.

I acquired the above set number 75045 in January of 2016 for $30. I sold it later that year for $90. Today, as of October 2019, the current price is $139.20.

I purchased set number 71308 for $9 in May of 2016. I sold it later that year for $39. Today, it's listed for $144.80. Keepa shows that it sold a month ago for $147. Where else can you buy for $9 and in 3.5 years sell for $147? Not many places.

LEGO Minecraft 21117 The Ender Dragon
by LEGO
★★★★☆ ~ 436 ratings | 19 answered questions

🔍 8 Price Changes

Price: **$195.52 & FREE Shipping**

Get a $125 Amazon.com Gift Card upon approval for the Amazon Business Prime Card. Terms apply.

Note: Not eligible for Amazon Prime. Available with free Prime shipping from other sellers on Amazon.

- Includes a Steve minifigure and 3 Endermen. Also includes 634 assorted LEGO pieces. Weapons include a sword and a bow
- Features a sand island, Ender Dragon, dragon egg, light-brick Ender Crystals, and obsidian pillar elements; Accessories include armor and a helmet
- The perfect gift for fans of LEGO building and Minecraft!
- Rebuild for more LEGO Minecraft creations! Add other biomes in the series to create your own LEGO Minecraft world!

I obtained the above set number 21117 for $35 in May of 2016. I sold it later that year in the $70 range. Today, it sells for $195.52.

LEGO Disney Princess Ariel's Undersea Palace
by LEGO
★★★★☆ ~ 139 ratings | 8 answered questions

🔍 5 Price Changes

Price: **$194.84** ✓prime **& FREE Returns**

Get a $125 Amazon.com Gift Card upon approval for the Amazon Business Prime Card. Terms apply.

- Features a palace with secret grotto, dressing room, trapdoor and slide, clam shell that opens and closes and a golden clam shell bed
- Accessories include a microphone, piano, trident, map, magnifying glass, lipstick, hairbrush, cake, coral, sea grass, shells and decorative stickers
- Create magical underwater adventures with the two mermaid sisters and their fishy friends
- Ariel's Undersea Palace measures over 9" (23cm) high, 9" (25cm) wide and 4" (12cm) deep
- Secret grotto measures over 2" (5cm) high, 1" (4cm) wide and 1" (3cm) deep

Compare with similar items

I secured the above set number 41063 for $21 in August of 2016. I sold several in December 2016 and January of 2017 for $90-100. Today, they go for just under $195.

I purchased the above set number 75916 for $14 in May of 2017. I sold it a year later for $49. Today, it goes for $91.

I bought the above set number 76103 for $17 in January of 2018. I sold it later that year for $43. Today, it goes for $115, with recent sales history around $130.

I purchased set number 70224 for $50 in November of 2017. I sold it a month later for $150. Today, it goes for just under $210.

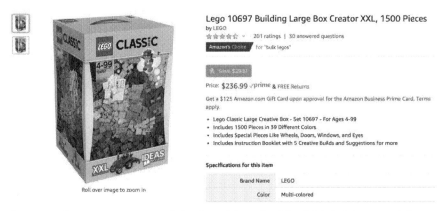

Set number 10697 was a Black Friday deal in 2016. You could find them at Wal-Mart for $30. What Wal-Mart didn't advertise, was that you could buy them for $50 in January 2017 on their website. I bought some at both price points and sold them in the $75-100 range later in 2017. Today, they sell well for $237.

I could go on and on to show you hundreds of examples in which the value of Legos has only increased over time. In fact, I have history of just over 400 Lego listings that I have never deleted from my seller history on Amazon. In those 400 plus listings, I could only count six examples where the current price was less than the price at which I sold. Four of those six are from sets that I purchased this year in 2019. Many of those are still available in retail stores and have more competition on them driving down price. In cases where the current price is under my sell price, the difference is minimal. In most cases it is less than a dollar and the most is less than five dollars. One of those original six examples comes from a set purchased in 2018 and the other from a set in 2017. Again, both are very close to my sale price. There were zero examples from 2016. The other 394 plus examples have all increased in value over the last several years.

Based on those 400 listings alone, if you buy right, there is nearly a 100% chance that you will make money. Even on the six listings where the price was less than my sale price, it doesn't mean that the price isn't profitable. It just means there is less profit to be made. At the very worst, those prices may be at a break-even point. While I hate to say something is a guarantee, because there are always outliers and circumstances that change, if you buy and hold Legos a couple years past your purchase date, you stand to potentially make exponential returns. That isn't just an opinion. That's five years of doing this and a 400 plus example case study on which I can look back and study.

Obviously, I still have much to learn about Legos, or better yet, must exercise more patience. For the last several years, my strategy has been to sell them within a year when I can at least make 100% ROI and keep cash flow moving. Moving forward, I will be trying to hold Legos for longer periods of time if capital allows. Your strategy is up to you. Whichever you choose, I hope your eyes have been opened to the idea of how Lego is a currency of its own and that you can profit from them in multiple ways.

Getting Ungated in Lego

On a monthly basis, I am asked how sellers on Amazon can get permission or ungated in Legos. I personally have never gone through the process as I was fortunate enough to be grandfathered in. However, the community of sellers I am in have had several success stories this year with newer sellers becoming ungated in the Lego brand. I am not going to write it here because it will probably change multiple times within the coming months and years. However, please join the Toyfolio Facebook group and I will be happy to explain the process that has currently worked. It may not work in the future, as Amazon loves to change things on a whim. If you want to get in on the action, please act quickly.

Miscellaneous Lego Tips and Resources

Most themed Lego sets come with what are called mini-figs. These are characters from whatever theme the set depicts. These characters can be highly sought after by collectors or even moms who have children that have misplaced them. Mini-figs can go for big money on eBay and sites like bricklink.com.

Mini-figs aren't the only thing you can pick out of a Lego set to resell. You can literally sell an entire set piece by piece. Each piece is numbered and again can be sold on sites such as eBay or Bricklink to collectors, novelists, and parents alike. Many times, these are people that have misplaced pieces or purchased incomplete sets that need these specific pieces in order to completely finish their project.

Obviously, parting out a complete Lego set takes some serious patience and determination. If that doesn't tickle your fancy (personally, it sounds awful to me), then you can sell loose and random pieces by the pound. I see these listings on eBay and Facebook Marketplace all the time. There are great profits to be made if you can find cheap, used sets or pieces and flip them on these sites.

8
TOYFOLIO EXAMPLES

You've seen several Lego examples, now I want to show you a few more Toyfolio examples to again show you the power of this strategy.

Roll over image to zoom in

Transformers Generations Titans Return Blitzwing and Decepticon Hazard
by Transformers
☆ ☆ ☆ ☆ ☆ ∨   54 ratings | 7 answered questions

Price: **$59.99** + $4.92 shipping

Get a $125 Amazon.com Gift Card upon approval for the Amazon Business Prime Card. Terms apply.

Note: Not eligible for Amazon Prime. Available with free Prime shipping from other sellers on Amazon.

- Voyager Class Blitzwing and Titan Master Decepticon Hazard figures
- Decepticon Hazard figure becomes the head for the Blitzwing figure
- Blitzwing figure is a Triple Changer figure
- Includes a collectible character card with tech specs
- Includes Voyager Class Blitzwing figure, Titan Master Decepticon Hazard figure, 2 weapon accessories, character card with tech specs, and instructions

Specifications for this item

Brand Name	Transformers

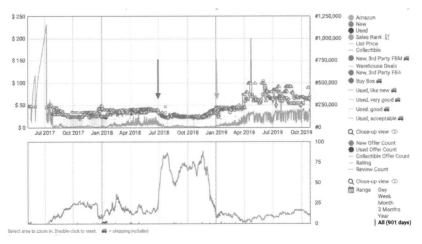

What you see on this page is a Transformers toy that I purchased from Ollie's last fall and summer. The graph you see above if you have not yet checked out the Facebook videos, is an example of a Keepa chart. I have inserted a red arrow on the chart to mark the point in time at which Ollie's came in stock. How do I know it came in stock there? Look at the bottom graph. That represents the number of offers or sellers on the listing. See how it spikes up? That's because this item was selling in the low to mid-$40 range and Ollie's had them for $12.99 (before any of their famous 10% and 15% off coupons).

What happens when the number of sellers goes from 14 to 87? The price literally cuts in half from $42 to $21. This is where sellers are making pennies, if anything. Many sellers that didn't find this item right away passed on it because when they found in later in the summer and in early fall, it was no longer very profitable. They passed on it and looked for different items. However, one look at the Keepa chart shows that this item sold well with a very good sales rank before it was discovered at Ollie's. Thus, knowing that "once they're gone, they're gone," at Ollie's, I drove around and bought over 100 of them and held onto them until a specific time, which is represented on the graph by the green arrow.

As expected, the price returned to its normal market price and

I sold all of them in the $35-50 range through December 2018 and the first part of 2019, profiting well over $1,000. Of the course, as of this year, they have continued to rise in price as the price as fluctuated between $60 and $90 most the year. This is because these are now impossible to find in stores yet demand for them on Amazon still exists. Someone out there somewhere is delighted that they can still find it at a price they are willing to pay.

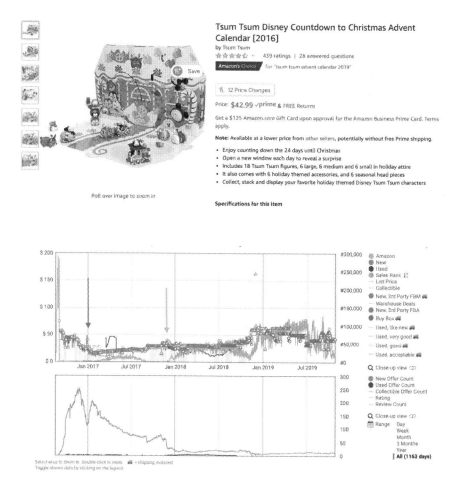

One of my favorite things to buy and hold every year are

advent calendars. These always spike and sell well during the holiday season. Surprisingly, they sell well throughout the year, but you won't find many on retail shelves until September, at the earliest. Retailers don't have a need to carry advent calendars most of the year and ones like the above example get marked down to $5 at Walmart. I purchased 100 of these in January 2017 because Keepa showed me that they sold very well in the $40 range just a couple months prior. The red arrow I have placed on the graph indicates when I purchased mine and you can see that several sellers jumped on the listing there and drove the price down to under $15. I held throughout the year and sold all of them for $35 apiece in November of 2017. As you can see, these went for nearly $70 in November of 2018. While they currently sell for $43, I expect them to spike and exceed $70 in November of 2019. After fees, I made around a $2,000 profit.

Roll over image to zoom in

Zoomer Dino, Jurassic world INDOMINUS REX-Collectible Robotic Edition
by Zoomer

★★★★☆ ˅   367 ratings | 30 answered questions

Price: $305.90 & **FREE Shipping**

Get a $125 Amazon.com Gift Card upon approval for the Amazon Business Prime Card. Terms apply.

Note: Not eligible for Amazon Prime. Available with free Prime shipping from other sellers on Amazon.

Product Packaging: **Standard Packaging**

- 6
- Imported
- The Hammond Creation Lab has made the most fearsome dinosaur ever displayed at Jurassic World. And now you can bring home the adventure of Jurassic World with the incredible Collectible Robotic Edition Zoomer Dino, Indominus rex.
- This Indominus rex uses True Balance Technology to hunt, patrol and explore its surroundings. Its advanced IR nose sensors detect your hand movements
- The Remote Control programs modes, records combo moves, and guide its movements. Each Indominus rex comes with a numbered Certificate of Authenticity

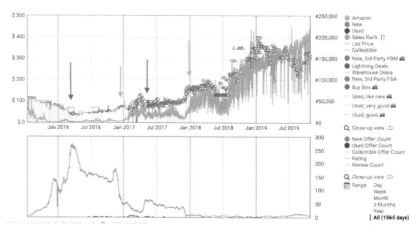

Jurassic World items are also some of my favorite items with which to build a Toyfolio. I have sold the Zoomer Indominus Rex toy twice over the past several years. I bought several for $20-30 in the spring of 2016 from Wal-Mart and Target, as indicated by the first red arrow, then sold them for $80 in December of 2016, which is indicated by the first green arrow. Prices went on to reach $120 after I sold mine, but before returning to the $70-80 range.

Since I knew that these sold well for $120 and that they had run their course in major retail stores and would not return, when I saw them available online from Kohls.com in the summer of 2017 for $60, I knew that this may be the last chance I'd ever have to be able to find them. I purchased 48 from Kohls that summer over the span of a month, because they would only allow me to order 6 at a time. Spacing the orders out also allowed to me to utilize the Kohls cash I earned and take advantage of other site-wide sales to lower my buy cost. I sold all 48 between $150-160 in December of 2017. As you can see, they have only increased in value since then.

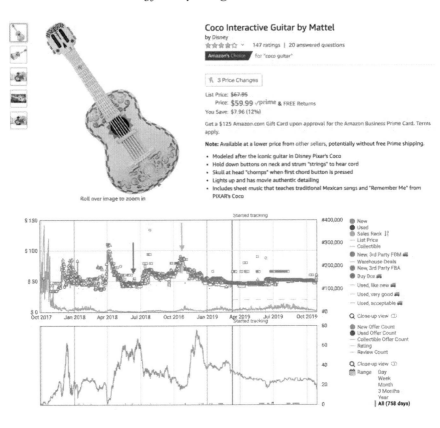

During the summer of 2018 Toys R' Us closed their doors for good. In doing so, they cleared out all of their inventory, which created a huge surge of inventory on the toy market. This Coco Guitar is one item that I bought all of them that I could find. MSRP was $34.99, so when these hit $17.50, I went all in. When I first found the guitars, they were selling in the $40 range, as indicated by the red arrow on the Keepa chart. There was some profit to be made, but not a ton, considering that the item is oversized and quite honestly, a pain to ship. Most sellers probably didn't want to deal with the aggravation for a smaller profit because these were some of the last items left on the shelves.

But, when I was in the stores, I was looking at Keepa chart. I saw that this toy had just sold for $80 in December of 2017 and for $100 around Easter 2018. Not only did it sell at those prices, but based on the Amazon sales rank, it sold quite well at those prices. Better yet, based upon my experience of spending time in all kinds of retail stores to buy inventory, I knew for a fact that I had never seen these toys in any other store...not even once. If Toys R' Us was getting rid of them, then that meant that in a matter of months, the only place you'd be able to find them would be online.

By Halloween of 2018 many sellers had sold out and I was selling these guitars for $85, as indicated by the green arrow. That's when the Disney Store came in stock online. They had them on sale for $30 and as you can see from the chart, a swarm of sellers jumped on the listing causing it to tank back to $50. I had to "settle" for selling my remaining inventory for $50-60 during Christmas and the first part of 2019. This was a lesson that things can always change and that sometimes, you have to adjust your plans and keep going. I was fortunate enough that I bought low enough and was still able to walk away with a nice profit. These are still available online through the Disney store as of the time of this writing. If they are ever discontinued (which they eventually will), the precedent has been set for them to be a winner.

littleBits Star Wars Droid Inventor Kit
by littleBits
★★★★☆ ▾ 501 ratings | 106 answered questions

🔥 3 Price Changes

List Price: $99.95
Price: $64.99 ✓prime & FREE Returns
You Save: $34.96 (35%)

Get a $125 Amazon.com Gift Card upon approval for the Amazon Business Prime Card. Terms apply.

- Now with coding! Kids learn how to control electronics with code in 6+ New Block-Based coding missions.
- Award-winning: winner of 50+ toy awards and gift guides, including creative toy of the year, Good Housekeeping & ttpm.
- Missions & challenges: now with 22+ missions in the app so kids can teach their Droid new skills.
- Customizable: missions help kids get creative, inventing new Droids & giving them personality.
- Requires Smart device: either iPhone (iOS 10.0 or later) or Android (KitKat 4.4 or later with Bluetooth 4.0 or later and an accelerometer) is required to build and control your Droid. Amazon devices not compatible at this time.

Roll over image to zoom in

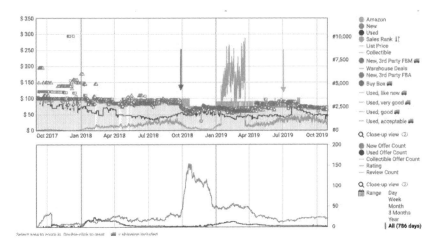

Last fall, Walmart put these Star Wars Droid Inventor Kits on clearance for $19. Yes, MSRP of $100 and on clearance for $19. My shopper and I found over 150 of them. As you can see, as indicated by the red arrow and the bottom graph, this is the time at which the number of sellers on the listing went from 28 to 150. This toy went from selling very well at $100 to $55 almost overnight. Remember, the orange shaded area means that Amazon is also in stock on this item. Contrary to what many sellers believe, you can compete and sell with Amazon on a listing. The proof is in the bottom graph. The graph wouldn't be going down if Amazon was not sharing the buy box. I sold many of these during the Christmas season in the $70 range and held the rest in anticipation that Amazon would go out of stock. As you can see, until the time of this writing they are still in stock. Fighting the urge to be greedy I again had to "settle" and sell these for $90 this summer, as indicated by the green arrow.

While I'll at admit that these examples are some of the best, a Toyfolio is much like a mutual fund or index fund. You will have some products that are homeruns, while others are going to do their job and earn you that consistent 30-40% ROI with very little work. Honestly, sometimes you will make bad buys or will be in a pinch for capital to spend. In these situations, yes, you could lose money. However, add them all together and spread your risk amongst them and you have a stable way to make a solid return on your investment.

In part, what made these purchases so good was the quantity I was able to secure. Buying something for $19 and selling it at a later date for $90 is nice, but multiplying that over 150 units is where the real magic happens. After you have learned this system and have proven to yourself that it is successful, I challenge you to go deeper in the quantities you buy. When you see winners based upon your market knowledge and it aligns with Keepa, you will be compelled to go find all you can and buy as many as you can afford. That skill and judgement will come with time. Today, all I want for you to do is to start. To start, buy toys an inch deep and mile wide, which simply means that you shouldn't put all your eggs into one toy. Don't expect to have a Toyfolio empire after day one. Taking small steps and actions will add up over time.

Toyfolio by Greg Webb

9
IS THIS A NOBLE THING TO DO?

In the five years that I have been doing retail arbitrage, I have experienced my share of funny looks when I'm pulling 3 full carts of baby dolls through stores. My favorite experience is when I am clearing a shelf of a particular item and it attracts the attention of other shoppers. Inevitably, I have a little grandma who comes over and asks me what the item is. After explaining what it is, people always must grab at least one and put it in their cart! Ten minutes ago, the same little grandma walked by that end cap and never even noticed the item. Ten minutes ago, little grandma didn't know what the item was! But now that I am clearing the shelf, she *had* to have one. People are funny.

I get all kinds of questions from other shoppers and cashiers. The most common questions, in no particular order, are as follows: Are you Christmas shopping early? Having a party? Do you have a bunch of kids? What are you going to do with all that? At times, I like to have fun answering these questions. Since I am buying and holding much of the inventory I purchase, I almost always answer the "early Christmas shopping," question with, "if you only knew," and just smile. If I'm not in the mood to have a long conversation, then the easiest response to most questions is, "something like that." However, the "what are you going to do with all that," requires a more in-depth response and I operate on the belief that honesty is the best policy.

I haven't always answered that question enthusiastically, more out of fear of getting into a debate, but recently I have been joyfully saying that I am a business owner and a seller on Amazon. In fact, I have noticed that when I just respond by saying, "I'm a reseller," I get more negative responses than if I say, "I am an Amazon seller." Essentially, they are the same response, but what is the difference? Amazon is the keyword. People have a positive view of Amazon. Why? Because of what I mentioned earlier in Chapter 2; Amazon is in the customer service business and they have gained the trust of millions of customers.

The keyword in that last sentence is *service*. When Amazon gets your package to you at a cheaper price than other stores or sites and saves you time by delivering it within two days, what have they just done? They have *served* you.

Now imagine the following scenario. It's a week before Christmas and you've been meaning to get to the store to get that special something for that special someone, but life is crazy. The kids have had some type of practice every night of the week. On top of that, you've had to go your office Christmas party, as well as your spouse's within the past week. You tell yourself that you're going to make the hour round trip to a cool store to get that gift over the weekend, but you just remembered that your in-laws are coming over to visit. Plus, the thought of driving in holiday shopping traffic and standing in those lines again gives you anxiety. Instead, you sit down with a cup of hot chocolate during the few minutes of peace you have after the kids have gone to bed and with a few clicks, from the comfort of your own home, you purchase that special something for that special someone on Amazon. While it was double what you would pay for it in the store, you didn't have to give up 2 hours of your day. You didn't have to spend the gas money to drive to the store or sit in traffic. You didn't have to leave your family or sacrifice something else in your busy schedule to make time to go to the store. Better yet, you were worried you'd get to the store and they would be sold out this late in the Christmas season, but Amazon had it in stock.

What did Amazon do in that situation? Did they rip your off because you paid double? Did they force you to buy the item? The answer to both is "no." You wanted the item and happily exchanged your money for not only the item, but also your time. Amazon guaranteed your item to you on time. It's a win-win for both parties.

As a third-party seller on Amazon, I am part of a group that supplies half of Amazon's inventory! Amazon and customers around the globe are counting on us to do what we do every day. Remember the discrepancy in the Snow Glow Elsa's from my county and Wake County, NC? That scenario plays out every year and year-round with multiple hot toys, but especially at Christmas. Thousands of parents and grandparents in the Wake County area depend on people like me to find the surplus hot toys in the rural areas around me and offer them on Amazon so that they don't have to participate in the rat race to find the item themselves. They don't want to drive hours around the state in hopes that maybe they will find the toy. They want to click a button and not think about it anymore.

One of the most confrontational encounters I've had was with a Wal-Mart cashier. He was furious that I was buying carts full of toys to resell. He would berate me anytime I would come through his line. He thought that buying and reselling items for a higher price was what the scum of the earth did. Now, I don't like confrontation and it's really hard to change someone's mind in a Wal-Mart checkout line, but the one question that he could never answer was "How does Wal-Mart make their money?" Hint: Wal-Mart buys inventory at a low price from various suppliers and they sell it for higher prices. No way! You mean that Wal-Mart (and every other business on the planet) does the same thing that I do? You betcha. All businesses need profit to survive. The best way I have ever heard it phrased comes from Daniel Lapin, who said that "profit is the applause people give you for serving them well." If you are making a profit, it is evidence that you have done something good, not bad. You have served your fellow man well with something that he or she valued more than the money in their wallet. Walmart serves their customers well and has for decades, or else they wouldn't still be in business today.

The question that almost always stopped the berating was "how does Wal-Mart afford to pay you," but he never answered, because I believe he knew the truth that I was helping pay him by purchasing items from that store. This is probably the biggest aspect of reselling that is missed by those that are against it. Reselling items on Amazon helps pay the salary of every employee at every store from which I buy inventory. It helps pay the salary of those who are working behind the scenes on the tools I use to find inventory. It helps pay those that provide my cell service and internet service as I work from home. It helps pay the USPS, UPS, and FedEx workers who pick up and drop off packages at my house most days of the week. It helps pay all of the Amazon workers that help my business run, from the warehouse workers that pack and ship items, to the customer service reps, to even those in higher positions that ensure Amazon runs smoothly.

I am serving customers by finding items that they want, and I am creating and sustaining jobs for people all around the country. This is how the economy works. We are all dependent on one another and everyone benefits from it! That sounds like a beautifully good thing to me, not something evil.

At the end of the day, you have to believe that what you are doing is a noble thing. If deep down you question yourself and what you are doing, you will jeopardize yourself and you won't work this business with the intensity that it needs. You will shy away from further opportunities and miss out on them in doing so. Rather, if you believe that what you are doing not only benefits you, but more importantly benefits everyone with whom you and your business comes in touch, will succeed exponentially.

All that to say, I hope you do believe in yourself and you don't just set this book aside and think that this was a neat concept. I want you to take action! There will be challenges and difficulties along the way, as everything in life worth doing also has. You don't have to know all the answers to get started, just take that first step and then take another. As the saying goes, "the best time to plant a tree was 20 years ago, the second-best time is now". Pretty soon you will find yourself fully immersed in this business and succeeding beyond what you ever imagined. I love to learn new things and I hope to one day learn something from you as we build our Toyfolios together.

Toyfolio by Greg Webb

10
CONTINUING THE TOYFOLIO CONVERSATION

This book is an attempt to broadly cover and reveal how I have built a Toyfolio over the past five years. I hope that it is sparking your interest and motivating you to pursue and build a Toyfolio for yourself.

I firmly believe that with this book and the free videos you'll find in the Facebook group, you will have all the tools necessary to start making money selling toys today. Your results depend 100% on you taking action though. I can answer a thousand questions in the group and will happily do so, but if you don't implement what you learn, then a Toyfolio won't build itself.

I find that many times when we try something new and challenging, we often get paralysis by analysis and we spend all of our time talking about what we want to do, learning about what we want to do, yet somehow, many of us never do what we want to do. For some of you, this has been an intriguing read, but at the end of the day, this just isn't your thing. I get it. No hard feelings. If there is anything I can do to help you navigate the world of online selling in the future, I will do my best to do so.

But for some of you, this book really resonated with you and you believe that you can build a Toyfolio. If that's you, then please get your feet wet and just start. Utilize what you have learned here and implement what you learn in the videos in the Facebook group. Sign up for the free version of Brickseek and Keepa and dive into the information. Do one thing a day and you will soon find yourself immersed in and seeing the trends that I see every day in the toy market.

While the group is brand new, my ultimate goal is that the free Toyfolio Facebook group can be a community where ideas and questions are shared by all of us that are on this journey together. You are a part of that. There is strength in numbers, and I believe that we are meant to help and serve one another. I hope that you can be a part of that and create the culture that I desire to see as we assist one another in this Toyfolio journey.

Other Facebook Groups

Sourceoholics BaLance Amazon FBA is the name of the Facebook group run by my good friends, Barrington and Lance. It is free and full of valuable content that will take your Amazon business to the next level. Join here:

facebook.com/groups/Sourceoholics/

Another free Facebook group I hang out in is **MySilentTeam Amazon FBA and Online Sellers**. This community can answer any online selling question you may have. I cannot say enough good things about the community Jim Cockrum and his team have built. Check them out here:

facebook.com/groups/mysilentteam/

Take a listen to Jim's podcast as well at:

silentjim.com/podcast/

Next Step

While I will be a part of the Toyfolio Facebook group and assist as many people as I possibly can, my first priority will continue to be the community that I have been serving via WhatsApp this entire year. For those who are unfamiliar with WhatsApp, it is a messaging app where hundreds can share content and conversations all from your computer or smartphone.

In this WhatsApp group, I post and share all of the Toyfolio deals that I am currently buying myself. Some of the other members of the group share their finds as well. People post items and frequently ask my opinion as to whether they should buy, sell, or hold. If anything, this group has helped me hone my Toyfolio skills over the past year as I am accountable to the group and want to provide them as much valuable content as possible. Every month, I host a webinar for this group where you can ask questions live and I can walk you through various buying and selling decisions step by step.

If you want to be a part of this group where I share toy buys and all the information I use to build a Toyfolio, then you can sign up at <u>buyandholdem.com</u>

The membership is $297 every quarter. Stay for one quarter, two, all year, or however long you'd like. There is absolutely no pressure to sign up at all. This group is only for those that want to know what I am personally buying and want to build a similar Toyfolio. If that doesn't interest you, then stay and hang out in the Toyfolio Facebook group for free as long as you'd like. We can still be friends and talk toys anytime.

One of my favorite testimonials for this WhatsApp group comes from Jaynie. She writes:

"I have learned so much from Greg Webb! His Buy & Hold strategies are business changing! His webinars on what type of products to look for, where/how to find them and how to interpret Keepa charts to know when to send them in are priceless! I have learned to look at sourcing in a whole new way. Before learning from Greg, I was familiar with Keepa and what the charts represented, but he taught me understand how that data can be used to know if a product is a good candidate for B&H. This year after implementing what I learned from him I have several replenishable products (that in the past I would have just given up on once the price tanked) that I just watch the prices and know when to wait and when to send them in to be profitable. I've also sourced a ton of clearance items that before I would have passed on - but thanks to what he's taught me I'm making crazy high ROI's by just waiting until the right time to sell. I recommend this training to anyone who wants to learn how to source and not worry about getting burned by the race to the bottom. Thanks Greg - you're awesome!!"

While Jaynie's words are kind, do you know what the greatest compliment Jaynie has paid me? She was a paying member of my WhatsApp group and left. Yes, leaving my paid group was a compliment. Why? Because she and her husband got it. They learned and implemented the strategies laid out here by taking massive action, and now they are doing this independently.

That too can be you. You just have to get started. What do you have to lose? I'd argue that it is riskier to not try to start making a side income and building something for yourself. If you are a W-2 employee somewhere, then you only have one customer. Your boss. You must keep that one customer happy all the time to continue to bring in income. With a Toyfolio, you have millions of customers. Would you rather have one customer or a million? I think you know the answer. Come, let's build a Toyfolio together!

Thank you

I want to personally thank you for taking the time out of your busy life to read my book. It truly is an honor. If you want to reach out, the best way to contact me is via email at toyfoliobook@gmail.com. Don't forget, you can find me in the Toyfolio Facebook group as well.

BONUS
A MONTHLY TOYFOLIO GUIDE

January:

Buying – This the month when most major retailers clear out massive quantities of toys. Most will be left over from Christmas, but some will be marked down to make room for new toys. Wal-Mart and Target go through their first clearance cycle at this time. Make sure you are checking regional stores as well. Ollie's will sometimes have a weekend where toys are marked down an extra 20%.

Selling – Many toys still sell at premium prices on Amazon in January because retailers have not yet caught up from the holiday rush and supply is still low. Don't get caught going too deep in a newer "hot," toy here. Many times, the market recovers and you're left holding a lot of inventory.

February:

Buying – This is the month where you can glean from all the clearance deals left over from January. It will require a little more work and hunting, but the deals and margins are better because for the most part, the deals are 70 to 75% off.

Selling – You can also sell a good amount of volume in

February due to Valentine's Day. This is when I like to start selling some of the deals I found on Black Friday and Cyber Monday.

March/April:

Buying – Quite honestly, these two months are the slowest months when it comes to finding new inventory. However, there are typically a few hot items that end up going for good money because there is an increased demand for toys around Easter.

Selling – There is a huge demand for toys around Easter. I typically have great sales during the two weeks leading up to it. This is also the time when I sell many of the items I bought on Black Friday and Cyber Monday. Most other sellers are sold out by this time. This is usually the first time I sell some of the items I purchased in January as well.

May/June:

Buying – The summer is quickly approaching and that normally means new kids' movies are being released. This means two things. One, that there are some hot, newly release toys related to the new movies that do well. Two, there are clearance items that are reduced to make room on the shelves for the new releases. I prefer option 2.

I've also had luck buying outdoor and water related toys during this time of year.

Selling – I have sold those same outdoor and water related toys in the same month. It's always nice to find inventory you can flip more quickly to keep capital flowing. Other than that, I'm mostly selling items I found earlier in the year.

July/August:

Buying – This is the second clearance cycle for major retailers like Wal-Mart and Target. I also like to say that if you don't make good purchases in July and August, then you are not going to have a good Q4. Target typically ends their clearance cycle by the end of July. Wal-Mart's clearance can push into the second or third week of August. Stores are having these massive clearance sales to make room for all the new inventory coming in for the Holidays.

Selling – Some items you find during these months are also items that you'll be able to sell right away. Other than that, I hope you are picking up on the pattern that I follow, which typically consists of constantly selling items I bought 3, 6, or 9 months ago.

September:

Buying – September is often the first look we get at all of the new toys that are coming out for holiday season. It's not really my style, but some of these hot new releases demand a premium from day one, until all stores have time to get stocked. During this time, you can see what I like to call the "new to market spike," on Amazon, where collectors and avid buyers pay double or triple the price just to get their hands on it.

Selling – If you do go after these toys mentioned above, my advice would be not to go too deep to avoid getting caught with a lot of stock when Amazon comes back in stock or retail supply catches up. Other than that, I boringly sell stuff I bought earlier in the year. Did I mention that I Buy and Hold stuff?

October:

Buying – For whatever reason, Wal-Mart especially has some really good clearance in October. Most of it is centered around the need to clear more shelf space for the movies being released in November and December. This is also the time during which I start hitting regional stores, such as Ollie's, hard. Other chain stores such as TJ Maxx, Ross, and others start receiving an increased supply of toys as well.

Selling – Many of the toys that I buy and hold could be used as an accessory to a Halloween costume, so this is when I sell them. I happen to be writing this paragraph in October of 2019 and many of my sales today came from a toy I purchased in December of 2018.

November:

Buying – By this point in the year, sellers generally know what is going to be hot for the Christmas season and what is not. Buy as much as you can afford. Cash sitting on the sideline can't make you money. As I have mentioned numerous times, I buy on Black Friday and Cyber Monday to flip items within a month like almost every other seller. However, I also tend to buy something with intentionality that I will sell in the future.

Selling – Black Friday and Cyber Monday. Need I say more?

December:

Buying – One of my favorite times to buy, as stores continue to have great sales. Sellers try to quickly flip those items and some end up tanking in price on Amazon. I love to continue to buy through the season and hold until Valentine's Day and Easter.

Selling – The 10-day window of December 12th to 22nd is typically the highest sales period of the year. More specifically, my highest sales day typically falls in the December 15th to 20th range for each of the last several years. Toys peak at insane prices each and every year during this window.